A GARDEN

SHRUBS
AND SMALL TREES

A choice selection of dependable plants for
year-round colour in the garden

Prunus 'Cheal's Weeping'

Buddleia davidii

A GARDENER'S GUIDE TO

SHRUBS
AND SMALL TREES

A choice selection of dependable plants for
year-round colour in the garden

NOËL PROCKTER

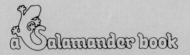

Published by Salamander Books Limited
LONDON

A Salamander Book

Published by Salamander Books Ltd.,
52 Bedford Row,
London WC1R 4LR.

© 1988 Salamander Books Ltd.

ISBN 0 86101 398 0

Distributed by
Hodder and Stoughton Services,
PO Box 6, Mill Road, Dunton Green,
Sevenoaks, Kent TN13 2XX.

All correspondence concerning the
content of this volume should be
addressed to Salamander Books Ltd.

Contents

Text and colour photographs are cross-referenced throughout as follows: 64♦. The plants are arranged in alphabetical order of Latin name. Page numbers in **bold** refer to text entries; those in *italics* refer to photographs.

Credits

Author: Noël J. Prockter is an experienced garden writer. Trained at Kew, he became manager of a leading plant nursery in southern England and then an Assistant Editor of 'Amateur Gardening' magazine. He has contributed to many radio gardening programmes and has authored several books and articles on a wide range of gardening subjects.

Editor: Geoff Rogers
Designer: Tony Dominy
Colour and monochrome reproductions: Tempus Litho Ltd., England.
Filmset: SX Composing Ltd., England

Printed in Belgium by
Henri Proost & Cie, Turnhout.

Introduction

Shrubs and small trees are either deciduous or evergreen, but all are perennial in as much as they do not die down in the autumn or winter like herbaceous perennials.

The majority of shrubs and trees are grown for their flowers, fruit or foliage and some trees are grown for all three. The Portugal laurel, *Prunus lusitanica*, has attractive dark glossy green foliage, slender racemes of dull white flowers plus a profusion of small purple cherry-like fruits. The pillar apple, *Malus tschonoskii*, has flowers in spring, followed by globose colourful fruits and even more brilliant foliage in autumn.

Other trees are sought after for their colourful and enchanting barks, such as the mahogany-barked cherry, *Prunus serrula* or the paperbark maple, *Acer griseum*, which peels to reveal a cinnamon-coloured bark beneath.

Some trees have graceful weeping habits, such as Young's weeping birch, *Betula pendula* 'Youngii', or the willow-leafed pear, *Pyrus salicifolia* 'Pendula', which bears white pear blossoms in spring while the silky white down on its foliage later changes to silvery grey; this and the weeping willows *Salix caprea* 'Pendula' and *S. purpurea* 'Pendula are ideal for the medium-sized or small garden.

Of the shrubs grown for their foliage what is more colourful than a bush of the golden elder, *Sambucus nigra* 'Aurea'? *Skimmia japonica* 'Foremanii' has bright scarlet berries and its white flowers are equally attractive; so, too, are the ruby red buds of *S.j.* 'Rubella'. The spidery golden-yellow fragrant flowers of the Chinese witch hazel, *Hamamelis mollis*, or the pendulous racemes of scented flowers of *Mahonia japonica* are both treats for a midwinter vase.

In summer, there are the delights of the fragrant mock oranges, *Philadelphus*, the lilacs, lavenders and rosemary. This compact guide presents a selection of trees and shrubs that provide colour and interest throughout the seasons.

Buying

When buying shrubs and trees endeavour to see that they are free of pests and diseases. Shrubs must be well rooted. As many will be purchased from garden centres, bear in mind that there are two

Left: **Pieris 'Forest Flame'**
What a splendid show this evergreen shrub puts on in spring. The newly emerging leaves are at first bright red, changing through shades of pink and orange to cream, and finally to green. At the same time, clusters of white flowers appear at the end of the previous year's shoots. 119♦

Right: **Paeonia suffruticosa 'Rock's Variety'**
These large semi-double flowers are borne on a slow-growing shrubby paeony up to 1.5m (5ft) tall. Grow in a rich well-cultivated soil. 117♦

types of container plant. Those that have been 'container grown' from cuttings, layers or seedlings and those shrubs and trees which have been lifted from the open ground and 'containerized'. Container-grown plants may be smaller or possibly more expensive, but they are usually more reliable. Standard trees should have sturdy stems; very thin-stemmed standard trees, known in the nursery trade as 'whips', can take a long time to fill out and make a decent stem.

Some nurserymen lift shrubs and trees direct from the open ground. Remember that severed roots may require trimming before they are planted. Plants without soil must have their roots spread out and placed in a planting hole large enough to prevent the roots from being cramped. Balled shrubs or trees, especially evergreens, with soil attached to their roots can be planted in their sacking if it is thin, but thick sacking should be removed. Polythene casing does not rot and must be removed once the shrub or tree is in position.

General cultivation
Remember that, once planted, a shrub or tree is likely to spend the rest of its days in the same spot. If possible, prepare the site some time before planting to allow the soil to settle. Ensure that the ground is thoroughly dug before planting. The best method is double digging. To do this, take out the first spit (spade's depth) of soil, break up the second spit (subsoil), and replace with the next spit of soil. If the ground is very poor, work in some well-rotted manure or well-rotted garden compost between the topsoil and subsoil. When planting in grass, leave a square or circle of ground

Above: **Camellia × williamsii 'Donation'**
Superb pink flowers in spring. 28♦

Left: **Laburnum × watereri**
Slender racemes of fragrant blooms adorn this tree in early summer. 92♦

without turf, about 1.2m by 1.2m (4ft by 4ft), so that air and moisture can reach the roots. Do not returf for at least four years.

Before planting, trim any torn or broken roots with a pair of sharp secateurs. At the time of planting, apply some bonemeal mixed with well-moistened peat (two handfuls per 9-litre/2-gallon bucket of peat). Spread this around the roots once a little soil has been returned to the planting hole. Bonemeal has the advantage of being slow acting, allowing the plants to make fresh roots.

Always plant firmly; nothing is more damaging to the roots of shrubs or trees than to be rocked by the wind, which can allow moisture to get in at the roots. Stake trees firmly and always insert the stake in the ground before the soil is returned to the planting hole to ensure that the roots will not be damaged. Preferably, stakes should be round; square ones can cause chafing to the bark, especially of trees. Use recognized tree ties, which can be purchased at any good garden centre. When planting shrubs and trees, do not forget that they will spread, so allow at least 1.2m (4ft) between each shrub. This will give them room to grow with the minimum of pruning. With a newly planted shrub, such as *Forsythia* or *Ribes* (flowering currant), prune back three or more shoots to within 30cm (12in) of the soil with sharp secateurs. This will encourage plenty of growth from the base.

Trees that have been budded or grafted at ground level may produce sucker growths from the stool or stock onto which the named variety has been worked. Such suckers must be removed, and if below ground, pulled away rather than cut; below the cut there are buds which can in time produce fresh suckers.

9

Propagation

Take most softwood cuttings in spring and insert them in a propagating frame with bottom heat or under a mist propagator. Take half-ripe cuttings during the summer months and root them in cooler conditions. The cuttings should be 5 to 10cm (2-4in) long, although heather cuttings need be only 2.5-5cm (1-2in) long. Take hardwood cuttings from mature shoots, usually of the current year's growth, during the autumn and winter. These cuttings should be 23 to 30cm (9-12in) long.

All cuttings should touch the base of the cutting hole or trench. Hardwood cuttings will survive in open ground throughout the winter even though they have calloused – ie formed a healing skin at the base of each cutting although no new roots will have started. With the arrival of spring, fresh roots will be emitted and there will be signs of growth above ground. To aid the establishment of soft and half-ripe cuttings, several root-promoting substances are available in powder form. Use these in accordance with the instructions.

Pests and diseases

Unfortunately shrubs and trees do not escape the ravages of pests, diseases and physiological disorders. The most common pests are aphids. These can affect *Berberis, Cistus, Deutzia, Euonymus, Ligustrum, Lonicera, Ribes, Pyracantha, Salix* and *Viburnum.* Control them by spraying with malathion or dimethoate. Capsid bugs perforate foliage and distort the shoots of buddleias,

Above: **Kerria japonica 'Pleniflora'**
These attractive double flowers appear in spring. In autumn the leaves turn to palest yellow. 90♦

Right: **Prunus subhirtella 'Pendula'**
A lovely specimen shows the full spring glory of this weeping tree. 124♦

forsythias and hydrangeas. A dimethoate spray is an effective control. Never use a chemical spray on a shrub in flower.

Several fungal and bacterial infections attack trees and shrubs. The shoots and flower buds of *Syringa*, for example, may be affected by a fungal disease called grey mould. Control this by spraying with a copper fungicide. Powdery mildew, particularly common on *Euonymus* and *Mahonia*, causes white deposits on the leaves and can be controlled by spraying with benomyl or dinocap. Silver leaf, a fungal disease that affects *Prunus* and some other species, produces a silvering of the foliage and purplish brown stains on diseased stems. Cut out affected shoots and paint the wounds with a fungicidal paint. Bud blast, a fungal infection of rhododendrons, kills the buds, turning them black, brown or silver in spring. Pick off any affected buds and burn them. Prevent the rhododendron leafhopper from spreading the disease by spraying with dimethoate or malathion. Fireblight, a serious bacterial infection, causes branches and shoots to wither and turn brown. It attacks *Chaenomeles*, *Cotoneaster*, *Crataegus* and *Pyracantha*. Control consists of cutting out the affected stems.

Physiological disorders can result from unsuitable cultural conditions. Bud drop on camellias, for example, can be caused by too dry a soil when the buds are forming. Prevent this by watering in dry periods and mulching in late summer and early autumn. Chlorosis, a yellowing of foliage, can affect hydrangeas grown in too alkaline a soil. Remedy this with peat and acid fertilizers.

Above: **Abelia × grandiflora**
These slightly fragrant flowers are produced freely in late summer. Grow in an open sunny spot. 17♦

Below: **Acer griseum**
The peeling bark is just one of the attractions of this medium-sized tree. Autumn foliage is red and orange. 17♦

Above: **Acer japonicum 'Aureum'**
In an open site this maple makes a
splendid specimen tree up to 6m
(20ft) in height. The bright yellow
foliage turns to shades of reddish
crimson in autumn. 18♦

Above: **Amelanchier lamarckii**
This close up reveals starry white flowers borne amidst the early spring copper-tinged foliage. 20♦

Below: **Amelanchier lamarckii**
In full spring bloom this ornamental tree justifies its common name of 'Snowy mespilus'. Grow in sun. 20♦

Above: **Acer palmatum
'Atropurpureum'**
This splendid display of colourful
foliage commends this maple for
garden use. Plant it in fertile soil and in
a sunny spot that offers shelter. 19♦

15

Above: **Arbutus unedo**
These delicate bell-shaped flowers appear amidst the glossy green foliage during the autumn months. 20♦

Below: **Aucuba japonica 'Variegata'**
This attractive foliage shrub thrives in sun or shady conditions. 22♦

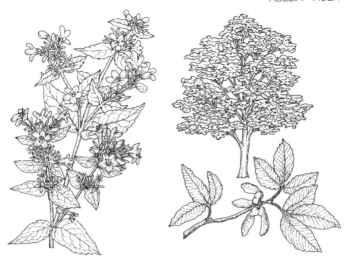

Abelia x grandiflora
- Open sunny spot
- Good loamy soil
- Late summer/early autumn flowers

This evergreen to semi-evergreen shrub will reach a height of 1-2m (3.3-6.5ft). Its slender arching branches are slightly downy; the striking, dark green foliage has smooth, pointed leaves, 2.5-6.5cm (1-2.5in) long, pale green beneath, more or less lightly toothed. The white pink-tinged funnel-shaped flowers have a faint fragrance, and are carried on the previous year's shoots in the leaf axils.

This hybrid has a good constitution and makes a vigorous graceful shrub, flowering late in the season. It does quite well on chalk and lime soils. Although there are several other abelias, A. x grandiflora is the most reliable. Endeavour to buy pot-grown plants.

Propagate by taking half-ripe cuttings in midsummer and insert them into a propagator with a little bottom heat.

Acer griseum
(Paperbark maple)
- Sun or light shade
- Most soils including chalk
- Superb autumn colour

This lovely small deciduous tree of Chinese origin is ideal for the small or medium garden, as it is slow-growing and takes many years to reach 7.6-9m (25-30ft). It is renowned for its charming peeling bark, which reveals a cinnamon-coloured layer beneath. Each heavily toothed leaf is composed of three leaflets. The green leaves are a pretty dove colour beneath. If I could choose only one tree for my garden it would be *Acer griseum*; no better choice could be found. In autumn the foliage is tinted superb shades of red and orange. This tree grows well on chalky soils and looks best when grown in a lawn, rather than in a border along with shrubs. When growing it in grass, be sure to allow ample cultivated ground around the base of the tree.

Although the Paperbark maple seeds fairly freely, the seeds have a very low germination rate.

Take care
Remove worn-out stems and very thin twigs in autumn. 12♦

Take care
Stake newly planted trees. 12♦

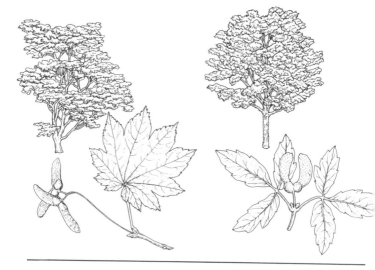

Acer japonicum 'Aureum'

(Downy Japanese maple)
- **Sunny position**
- **Most soils, including lime**
- **Foliage throughout the season**

An acer worthy of note is the deciduous Downy Japanese maple, especially the cultivar 'Aureum'. The species *A. japonicum* has typical maple leaves, each with seven to 11 lobes. In spring, before the foliage appears, purplish red flowers are produced. In autumn the foliage turns to tones of rich reddish crimson, providing a stunning display in the garden. It will make a tree 6-9m (20-30ft) high.

The cultivar 'Aureum' rarely grows higher than 6m (20ft), and even then it grows slowly. Its lobed foliage is a pale golden to bright yellow throughout the season. It is a superb small tree or large shrub for the small or medium-sized garden, and has the advantage of growing well on chalk soils. Propagate *A. japonicum* by seed in early spring, and 'Aureum' by budding or grafting.

Take care
Shelter *A. japonicum* and the cultivar 'Aureum' from cold winds and late frost, which can damage foliage. 13♦

Acer nikoense

(Nikko maple)
- **Sun or dappled shade**
- **Moist soils including chalk**
- **Late spring flowers; autumn foliage**

A deciduous tree from Japan and central China eventually reaching a height of 6-7.6m (20-25ft). Although said to be at its best when planted in woodland conditions or where it can have dappled shade, it is nevertheless equally at home as a specimen tree on a lawn. The dark green leathery trifoliate leaves are covered with bristly hairs; the branchlets are also hairy. In late spring, after the foliage has formed, yellow flowers are borne in bunches of three grouped together, carried on drooping hairy stalks. In autumn the foliage provides a beautiful display as the leaves turn to shades of crimson and rich bronze-red or yellow. In winter the tree is adorned with attractive long pyramidal buds.

Propagate this tree by seed, sown under glass in a cool house in late winter.

Take care
Any pruning necessary should be done in summer or early autumn.

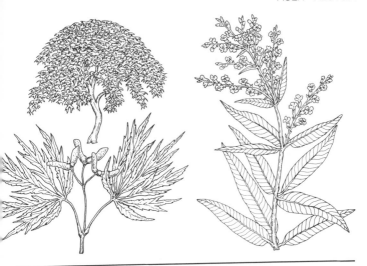

Acer palmatum 'Atropurpureum'

- **Sun or partial shade, sheltered**
- **Good loamy or peaty soil**
- **Foliage spring, summer and autumn**

The species *A. palmatum* seeds freely and many forms have been raised, among them many shades of colouring and some with finely cut foliage. the superb cultivar 'Atropurpureum' rarely reaches more than 4.5m (15ft). It has five-lobed leaves, or sometimes seven-lobed. When the sun shines through the foliage, rich reddish purple tints are seen during spring and summer. In autumn the foliage becomes bright red before it falls. Sometimes the leaves get cut by late spring frosts, but they soon recover.

This lovely maple needs a well-drained loamy or peaty soil. A sunny site suits it best and in spring it needs protection from cold winds. To be seen at their best, bushes need to be planted with a background of dark green foliage such as Portugal laurel.

Propagate by seed in spring or by budding in early summer. When pruning is necessary do it in late summer or early autumn.

Take care
Do not crowd plants. 15♦

Aloysia triphylla
(Lemon-scented verbena)

- **Full sun**
- **Any good soil**
- **Scented foliage late spring and autumn**

This deciduous shrub has also been known as *Verbena triphylla, Aloysia citriodora* and *Lippia citriodora*. Few people can resist rubbing their hands against the 7.5-10cm (3-4in) lance-shaped fragrant foliage. Lemon-scented verbena needs mild conditions, but is well worth the trouble for its scented leaves. The small pale purple flowers in late summer are insignificant.

Because this is a semi-tender shrub, each winter some young growths are likely to be killed. When this happens, prune them back to live wood in spring when buds start to show signs of life; often it will be necessary to cut shoots back to older wood. Although this aloysia is more often than not grown against a wall or fence, it can form an interesting feature in a border among shrubs in milder localities.

Propagate this shrub by softwood cuttings during the summer.

Take care
Plant out in spring from pots.

Amelanchier lamarckii

(Snowy mespilus)
- **Full sun**
- **Any good soil including lime**
- **Spring flowers; autumn foliage**

This small deciduous tree or large shrub has for a long time been erroneously identified as *A. canadensis* or *A. laevis*. When grown as a small tree it needs to have a main stem about 1.2-1.5m (4-5ft) before the branches start. If grown as a large shrub it can have several stems from the base. But either tree or shrub is exactly right for a small or medium-sized garden. The eventual height of a tree will be approximately 4.5-6m (15-20ft), sometimes more.

In spring the unfurling silky oval leaves have a coppery to pinkish hue. Before the foliage changes to a yellowish dark green, clouds of starry white flowers are scattered among the branches. Finally, in the autumn, there is a breathtaking display of orange and red foliage.

Propagate by seed, which should be sown as soon as it has been gathered, or by grafting in spring.

Take care
With standard trees, young shoots may appear up the main stem; rub these off to retain a clean stem. 14♦

Arbutus undedo

(Strawberry tree)
- **Full sun**
- **Good fertile soil, including lime**
- **Autumn flowers and fruits**

This tree or large shrub 4.5-9m (15-30ft) high, is surely one of the most beautiful flowering evergreens. Often trees have a gnarled appearance, and the old dark brown bark shreds as trees become established. The glabrous leaves are a dark shining green, leathery and toothed, 5-10cm (2-4in) long, narrowly oval and tapering towards each bud. *A. unedo* will grow where lime is present, which is unusual for ericaceous plants. It also grows well near the sea, where it often fruits more freely.

The white pitcher-shaped flowers are freely borne in early and mid-autumn, and often well into winter; at the same time round orange-red strawberry-like fruits appear. The fruits are very gritty and unpalatable.

Propagate by seed sown in spring, or by cuttings of the current year's wood taken during winter and placed in a propagating frame.

Take care
If trees or bushes are damaged by severe weather, prune them back hard when new growth starts. 16♦

Aronia arbutifolia
(Red chokeberry)
- **Full sun**
- **Good fertile soil; not chalk**
- **Spring flowers; autumn foliage and fruits**

A colourful deciduous shrub that makes a vigorous, spreading bush. For perfection, it needs ample strong young wood from the base. Bushes reach 1.5-2.5m (5-8ft) under ideal conditions, but not on shallow chalk or lime soils. It has narrow oval glossy leaves, tapered at each end 4-9cm (1.6-3.5in) long and 1-2cm (0.4-0.8in) wide. In spring it has white flowers with a slight rosy tinge, followed in autumn by pear-shaped red berries and brilliant red foliage.

To ensure plenty of young shoots from the base, older branches need to be cut out, provided there is enough young growth. This should be done after the autumn foliage and fruit are over, ideally in late winter.

Propagate by seed sown in the open in spring, by suckers in early spring, or by half-ripe cuttings in early summer.

Atriplex halimus
(Tree purslane)
- **Sunny position**
- **Any soil**
- **Foliage most of the year**

This semi-evergreen shrub, in cultivation since the 17th century, is grown for its attractive silver-grey foliage. It looks most effective planted in association with dark green shrubs. The alternate leaves are 1-6.5cm (0.4-2.5in) long and 6mm-2.5cm (0.25-1in) wide.

For anyone who gardens near the sea, tree purslane is especially useful as a screen against sea winds. Provided it is planted in well-drained manured soil, even chalk or lime, it will flourish and repay the attention given to it. Sometimes severe frosts damage the foliage, but spring pruning puts matters right and new growth is soon produced.

Propagate by half-ripe cuttings in midsummer, or by hardwood cuttings in autumn.

Take care
Be sure to encourage young growth from the base of the plant.

Take care
Prune back frost-damaged bushes in spring for healthy new growth.

21

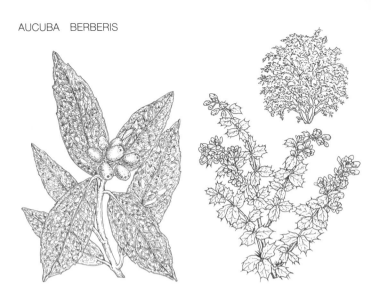

Aucuba japonica 'Variegata'

- Shade or sun
- Any good soil, including lime
- Spring flowers; summer and autumn fruits

An evergreen, 2-3m (6.5-10ft) tall, with glossy yellowish spotted green foliage. The cultivar 'Variegata', introduced from Japan in 1783, is sometimes known as *A.j.* 'Maculata', but the true 'Maculata' is a male form whereas 'Variegata' is female. Its small purplish flowers produce oval-shaped scarlet berries, provided there is a male form to effect pollination. Both foliage and berries are useful for flower arranging.

In order to have plenty of good young growth, give an annual mulch of leaf mould, but do not fork over the ground beneath the bushes. If necessary, pruning is best carried out in early spring, and when needed a few old growths can be cut back to about 60cm (24in) above ground level.

Propagate by hardwood cuttings 15-23cm (6-9in) long, in autumn, inserted out of doors.

Take care
Use sharp secateurs to prune. 16♦

Berberis darwinii

(Darwin's barberry)

- Sunny position
- Good fertile soil
- Spring flowers; autumn fruits

A lovely flowering evergreen that reaches a height of 2-3m (6.5-10ft). Its shield-shaped leaves are dark green, glossy and stalkless. It was discovered in Chile by Charles Darwin in 1835. In spring bushes are covered with deep orange-yellow flowers tinged with red, on drooping racemes 4-5cm (1.6-2in) long. In late summer to early autumn, oval plum to bluish coloured berries are produced.

It is perfectly hardy, but should be given a position sheltered against drying winds. It does best in moist fertile soils, including chalky ones. Prune, if necessary, in spring or after the bushes have flowered, using sharp secateurs.

Propagate by seed sown in late winter in a prepared seed-bed out of doors, or take half-ripe cuttings in late summer.

Take care
Do not allow to get too dry. 34♦

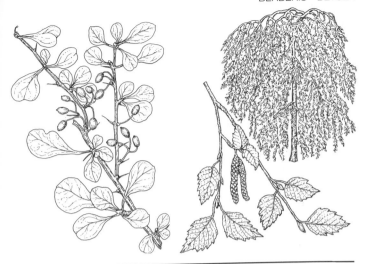

Berberis thunbergii
(Thunberg's barberry)
- **Sunny position**
- **Tolerates most soils**
- **Spring flowers; autumn foliage and fruit**

This hardy deciduous shrub is popular not only for its compact habit, but also for its red fruits and brilliant red foliage in autumn. Bushes reach a height of 1-2.5m (3-8ft) and the same width. The stiff grooved shoots have reddish brown bark. In spring, small red and yellow flowers are freely borne. Its stiff single thorns, sometimes three-pronged, are 1cm (0.4in) long, and very hurtful.

Various forms, cultivars, varieties and hybrids have been produced. *B.t.* 'Atropurpurea' has rich reddish purple foliage in spring and summer, becoming more intense as autumn approaches. 'Atropurpurea Nana' is a useful low shrub, about 60cm (24in) high. 'Rose Glow' has purple foliage variegated with pink and white.

Propagate by seed sown as soon as ripe or in late winter; by half-ripe cuttings in summer; or by hardwood cuttings in autumn.

Take care
Wear strong gloves when pruning in late winter, if thinning is necessary.

Betula pendula 'Youngii'
(Young's weeping birch)
- **Open sunny situation**
- **Light sandy fertile soil**
- **Winter/spring catkins; autumn foliage**

Here is a perfect weeping tree for a small or medium-sized garden. In spring its weeping branches display the yellow pendent male catkins, which in winter are greenish. The erect female catkins are pale green, enhanced by small dull crimson stigmas. The slender branches are pendulous, and specimens trained with a leading stem or grafted onto a standard stock of *Betula pendula* (Silver birch) 1.5-2m (5-6.5ft) high produce a dome-shaped tree.

Young trees need staking until they are strong enough to stand on their own. Avoid thin chalky soils; although trees will thrive on fairly fertile soil where lime is present, undoubtedly this weeping birch, like other birches, grows better on lime-free soils. Avoid very wet ground, too.

Propagate by grafting in late winter under glass; or by budding in midsummer out of doors onto stocks of *Betula pendula*.

Take care
Stake young trees securely.

23

Buddleia alternifolia

- **Open sunny situation**
- **Good loamy soil**
- **Summer flowers**

This small deciduous weeping tree has lance-shaped, dark green leaves 4-10cm (1.6-4in) long and 6-12mm (0.25-0.5in) wide. The bright lilac-purple flowers are slightly fragrant, and a well-grown tree with the main stem securely staked makes a delightful sight in full bloom during the summer. One of the best specimens I have seen at the Royal Horticultural Society's garden at Wisley, England, is said to be over 50 years old.

To maintain a healthy specimen, cut out the old flowered shoots as soon as the flowers have faded; at the same time, remove any dead or unwanted shoots. Standard trees usually have a main stem 1-1.2m (3.3-4ft) high. On established trees remove all surplus shoots that appear on the main stem.

Propagate by half-ripe cuttings taken during the summer.

Take care
Remove old flowering shoots. 33♦

Buddleia davidii

(Butterfly bush)
- **Sunny location**
- **Any good soil**
- **Summer flowering**

The common name of this deciduous summer-flowering shrub is derived from its attraction to butterflies. *B. davidii* grows to a height of 3 to 4m (10-13ft) and the four-angled stems make widespreading bushes with an open habit. The lance-like leaves are dark green above and white-felted beneath. The fragrant flower trusses cluster in tapering panicles 15-75cm (6-30in) long.

There are many varieties to choose from: 'Black Knight' is dark purple; 'Harlequin', reddish purple with creamy white variegated foliage; 'Peace', pure white; and 'Royal Red', purple-red.

Annual pruning needs to be done during late winter; cut back the previous year's growth to within a few buds. Newly planted bushes should have their growths pruned to half their length for the first two or three years.

Propagate by half-ripe cuttings in summer, or by hardwood cuttings in autumn.

Take care
Prune annually in late winter. 34-5♦

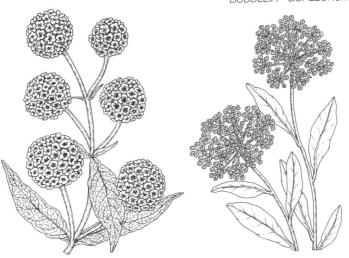

Buddleia globosa
(Orange ball tree)
- **Sunny location**
- **Any fertile soil, including lime**
- **Early summer flowering**

The almost evergreen Orange ball tree is a striking shrub, with orange-yellow ball-like flowers and dark green wrinkled foliage; the downy covering above and tawny felt covering beneath are outstanding. The lance-shaped leaves are 13-20cm (5-8in) long and 4-5cm (1.6-2in) wide. The honey-scented globose flowers, each about 2cm (0.8in) in diameter, are carried in terminal panicles of eight to ten; each panicle can measure 15-20cm (6-8in) long. Well-grown shrubs can reach 4.5m (15ft) in height and spread.

Only in very hard winters will this buddleia become a semi-deciduous shrub; certainly in milder localities it will remain evergreen. Pruning usually entails cutting out all weaker shoots in spring. When they become too large, bushes can be cut hard back in early spring, but flowers will be lost for one season.

Propagate by half-ripe cuttings in early to mid-summer.

Take care
Keep bushes in good shape. 35♦

Bupleurum fruticosum
- **Sunny position**
- **Any good soil, including lime**
- **Flowers midsummer/early autumn**

This hardy evergreen or semi-evergreen flowering shrub has a rather floppy habit, and grows 1.5-2.5m (5-8ft) high. It is a must for seaside areas and for those who have to garden in chalky soils. Its small yellow flowers are borne on terminal umbels 7.5-13cm (3-5in) across, and carried on purplish young shoots. The alternate narrow blue-green leaves are 5-9cm (2-3.5in) long and 2-4cm (0.8-1.6in) wide.

When the bush becomes untidy and thick, cut it hard back to within about 15cm (6in) of the ground in late spring; by autumn it will have become a shapely bush again. With such treatment a season's flower display will be lost, but the result will be rewarding.

Propagate by taking firm side shoots and inserting them in a cold frame in late summer.

Take care
Keep these evergreen bushes in good shape by regular pruning.

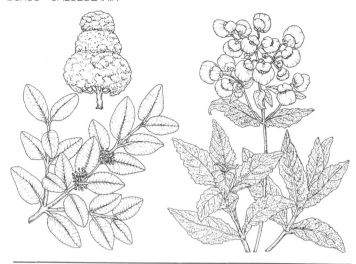

Buxus sempervirens
(Box)
- **Sun or dappled shade**
- **Well-drained, chalky soils**
- **Spring flowering**

This hardy evergreen shrub can be grown as a large spreading bush or as a small tree 4.5-6m (15-20ft) tall or more. The oval dark green shining leaves, notched at the apex, are 1-2.5cm (0.4-1.0in) long and half as wide. In spring the musky pale green flowers with yellow anthers are a glorious sight. *B. sempervirens* has many uses: it hides unsightly places, tolerates half-shaded situations, and can be trimmed into topiary. When bushes are overgrown cut them back to within 15-30cm (6-12in) of ground level. To encourage new growth give a feed of general fertilizer and a mulch of well-rotted garden compost. Edging box, *B. sempervirens* 'Suffruticosa', is ideal for low hedges of about 1m (39in) high.

Propagate by cuttings (side shoots with a heel) in late summer or early autumn, or divide 'Suffruticosa' during the spring.

Take care
Keep bushes and edging in good shape by regular pruning.

Calceolaria integrifolia
- **Sunny situation**
- **Well-drained, loamy soil**
- **Summer flowering**

The mention of calceolarias makes many gardeners think of tender plants with pouched flowers. *C. integrifolia* is a bushy shrub about 1.2m (4ft) tall. Its sage-like opposite dull green leaves, 5-9cm (2-3.5in) long and 2-4cm (0.8-1.6in) wide, have a soft greyish felt beneath and are stalkless. The pouch-like, bright yellow flowers grow in terminal flat-topped clusters during summer.

Although tolerably hardy in many areas, this shrub appreciates protection from a wall, fence or hedge, and an aspect warmed by the sun. In cold districts, cover plants with dry bracken against frost damage. Even with these reservations, however, it is a worthwhile and attractive shrub.

Prune in spring if plants have been damaged during winter. If it is severely cut back, this charming shrub will soon break freely from any live wood. Propagate it by softwood cuttings in summer.

Take care
Protect this sun-loving shrub. 36♦

Callicarpa bodinieri
(Beauty berry)
- **Sunny position**
- **Well-drained fertile soil**
- **Summer flowers, autumn fruit and foliage**

An unusual deciduous shrub that grows 1.5-2.5m (5-8ft) high, though mature bushes may spread their branches horizontally. The oval or lanceolate dark green leaves are 5-13cm (2-5in) long and 2.5-5.7cm (1-2.25in) wide, and the underside is paler and downy. The lilac flowers, freely produced in midsummer on leafy shoots, are followed by deep lilac to violet-blue fruits. In the autumn the whole shrub is aflame with deep rose-purple or violet-purple foliage.

If the bushes grow out of shape, cut them well back as new growth starts in spring. New growth will also arise from the base.

Propagate by cuttings, about 10cm (4in) long; sever strong tips below a node (leaf joint), and insert them in a moist cuttings mix in a cold frame during summer.

Take care
Remove any dead or frosted wood when new growth starts in spring.

Calluna vulgaris
(Common Heather; Ling)
- **Open sunny situation**
- **Any fertile lime-free soil**
- **Flowers from summer to late autumn**

This species can be found growing on moorland and mountains over a wide area in Europe. Today there are many cultivars and varieties, in a wide range of colours, with single or double flowers. Of the doubles, the 23cm (9in) 'J.H. Hamilton' has bright pink flowers from late summer to early autumn. An old favourite is 'H.E. Beale', 60cm (24in) tall, with sprays of soft pink flowers in autumn; on some soils it may be difficult, but on clay soil it does well. 'Gold Haze' is 60cm (24in) tall, with golden foliage and sprays of white flowers; and 'Cuprea', only 30cm (12in) tall, has coppery foliage and light mauve flowers in late summer to early autumn.

Prune these heathers when flowering has finished by cutting off old flowerheads; but if they are grown for foliage, cut off the dead flower spikes in spring.

Propagate by taking heel or nodal cuttings in summer, or by layering during the spring.

Take care
Ensure added peat is moist.

27

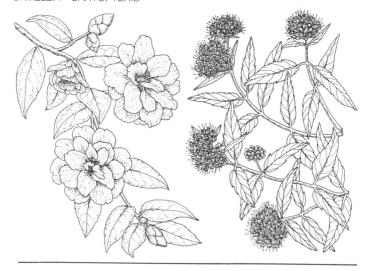

Camellia × williamsii 'Donation'

- Sun or partial shade
- Good acid or neutral peaty soil
- Spring flowers

These handsome evergreen shrubs are quite hardy, except that their flower buds and flowers can be damaged by frost. Although camellias do well in partial shade, they do equally well in full sunshine. Their hate is lime soils. They need an ample supply of sifted leaf mould or peat.

Today there are many varieties of *C. japonica* but for the small or medium-sized garden there is nothing more beautiful than *C. × williamsii* 'Donation'. Its soft pink semi-double flowers, about 13cm (5in) across, are borne above dark green glossy foliage. The growth is vigorous and erect, reaching a height of 2-3m (6.5-10ft).

Prune camellias when bushes become overgrown; they can be cut hard back after flowering has finished. Otherwise the only pruning needed is to keep bushes shapely.

Propagate by half-ripe cuttings of the current year's wood during the summer under glass.

Take care
Moisten peat properly before use. 37♦

Caryopteris × clandonensis

(Blue spiraea)
- Sunny position
- Any good fertile soil
- Autumn flowering

This attractive deciduous flowering shrub 1-1.5m (3.3-5ft) high and 1.2-2m (4-6.5ft) wide, forms a group of hybrids derived from the crossing of *C. incana* and *C. mongolica*. The cultivar 'Arthur Simmonds' has lance-shaped leaves rounded at the base, 3.5-6.5cm (1.4-2.5in) long, wrinkled and dull green above, silvery-grey beneath; sometimes there are one or two outstanding teeth near the top of the leaves. Clusters of blue flowers are borne in the axils. 'Arthur Simmonds' makes a neat rounded bush about 60cm (2ft) high. The cultivar 'Kew Blue' is darker.

Caryopteris is hardy in most areas, but may be damaged by frost in very hard winters. Nevertheless it needs hard pruning nearly to the base each spring. New bushes need a little protection from frost; cover them with small wigwams of canes or sacking.

Propagate by softwood cuttings during midsummer, or by half-ripe cuttings in late summer.

Take care
Protect newly planted bushes. 37♦

Cassinia fulvida

(Golden heather)
- **Sun or dappled shade**
- **Any good soil, including lime or chalk**
- **Summer flowering**

This erect heath-like evergreen shrub, up to 2m (6.5ft) tall, has closely packed branches covered with small slightly sticky leaves, dark green above, yellowish and downy beneath. In summer small white flowers are borne in dense terminal heads, 2.5-7.5cm (1-3in) across.

This wind-hardy shrub is especially suited to coastal areas. It is a native of New Zealand and should survive all but the most severe of winters. Grow it in full sun or dappled shade and ensure that the soil is fertile and well drained. From time to time, hard pruning will be needed to correct bushes that have become untidy or weak-stemmed; this should be done in spring.

Propagate by cuttings, using mature shoots 10-15cm (4-6in) long, in late summer or early autumn.

Take care
Keep these evergreen bushes in good shape by regular pruning.

Catalpa bignonioides 'Aurea'

(Golden Indian bean tree)
- **Sunny, sheltered situation**
- **Any fertile well-drained soil**
- **Summer and autumn foliage**

The golden form of *Catalpa bignonioides*, 'Aurea', is grown for its beautiful foliage. This deciduous tree is more often grown as an outsized bush, and can reach 7.6m (25ft) or taller. When grown as a standard tree, 'Aurea' is grafted onto stocks of *C. bignonioides*.

The species *C. bignonioides* has foxglove-like panicles of flowers that are frilled around the edges, and speckled with purple and yellow. These flowers are followed by bean-like seedpods. The magnificent heart-shaped golden leaves of *C.b.* 'Aurea' are pointed at the tip, and are 10-25cm (4-10in) long and 8-20cm (3.2-8in) wide. Fortunately the yellow foliage does not become green or dull as the season advances.

Propagate the species by seeds sown under glass in late winter, or out of doors in spring; or by half-ripe shoots under mist spray in late summer. Prune in winter or early spring.

Take care
Plant young bushes or trees. 38-9▶

Ceanothus × delinianus

(Californian lilac)
- **Sunny sheltered situation**
- **Any good fertile soil including lime or chalk**
- **Summer to autumn flowering**

Ceanothus × *delinianus* and its varieties form a group of deciduous shrubs which reach 1.5-2m (5-6.5ft) tall; most have blue flowers but a few are shades of pink. 'Gloire de Versailles' has enormous panicles of powder-blue flowers; 'Topaz' has bright indigo-blue flowers; and 'Henri Desfosse' is a darker blue than 'Gloire de Versailles'. 'Marie Simon' is rose-pink, and 'Perle Rose' is carmine-rose.

The panicles of flowers are produced on the new wood and for this reason bushes must be hard pruned each year in spring; cut plants back almost to the base of the previous year's growth. To encourage good growth, feed with a general fertilizer and mulch with well-rotted leaf mould, good garden compost or farmyard manure (but it must not be fresh).

Propagate in summer by half-ripe cuttings of the current year's growth.

Take care
Prune each spring. 38▶

Ceanothus impressus

(Californian lilac)
- **Sunny position**
- **Any good fertile soil, including chalk**
- **Spring flowering**

This evergreen shrub has clusters of deep blue flowers in spring, but even before the flowers open, the dark red flower buds are attractive. The almost rounded leaves, 6-10mm (0.25-0.4in) long, are dark green and deeply furrowed, and paler green beneath. This species makes a low-growing shrub about 1.5m (5ft) high and equally wide.

This is one of the hardiest of the evergreen ceanothus species. Even if a treasured specimen is killed by hard frost, they are easily propagated, and provided a few cuttings are taken from time to time, young plants can soon replace the loss. After it has flowered, shorten the longest shoots; do this ever year.

Propagate by half-ripe cuttings of the current year's growth in late summer

Take care
Have a stock of young plants available in case of losses. 38-9▶

Cercis siliquastrum

(Judas tree)
- **Full sun**
- **Any well-drained soil**
- **Mid- to late spring flowering**

Legend says it was on this tree that Judas hanged himself after the betrayal. Whether this is correct or not, the sight of its clusters of purplish-rose flowers is unforgettable. They are produced in spring from the joints of the old wood and on the trunks of old trees.

This deciduous tree or outsized bushy shrub reaches up to 7.6m (25ft) in height, and trees nearly 100 years old will be about 9m (30ft) tall. The roundish leaves are as attractive as the flowers, each having a heart-shaped base, green above and greyish green below. In midsummer the flowers are followed by pea-shaped pods, 7.5-13cm (3-5in) long.

This species will thrive in well-drained soils, and prefers a milder climate rather than a cold hard one. Propagate by sowing seed under glass in late winter or early spring. Remove dead wood in late winter.

Take care
Transplant at an early stage, as older plants resent disturbance. 40♦

Chaenomeles × superba 'Knap Hill Scarlet'

(Japanese quince; Japonica)
- **Sunny situation**
- **Any good well-drained soil**
- **Spring flowers; autumn fruits**

For a stunning display of bright red flowers throughout the spring months it is hard to beat this superb deciduous shrub. The cup-shaped flowers, each 2.5-4cm (1-1.6in) across, are borne in clusters on spiny twigs clothed in the new spring foliage. During the autumn these give way to golden yellow edible fruits, the quinces. Bushes grow to a height of about 1.2-1.5m (4-5ft) and as wide.

Other quinces to look out for are *Chaenomeles × superba* 'Crimson and Gold', which forms a dense spreading shrub about 1m (39in) tall, and the many varieties of *Chaenomeles speciosa*, particularly 'Simonii', which bears semi-double bright crimson-scarlet flowers on a slow-growing shrub to 75cm (30in).

Propagate all these shrubs by seeds sown in spring, by half-ripe cuttings in summer, or by hardwood cuttings in late autumn or winter. Little pruning is necessary except thinning.

Take care
Keep bushes neat and tidy.

Chimonanthus praecox
(Winter sweet)
- **Sun or light shade**
- **Any fertile soil, except acid ones**
- **Flowers from midwinter**

This deciduous sweetly scented shrub is often seen growing beside a wall or fence, but it can be grown as a compact free-standing shrub, reaching a height of 2.5m (8ft) and equally wide. The lance-shaped leaves, 5-13cm (2-5in) long, are a dark lustrous green and rough when handled. Its solitary fragrant flowers, 2-3cm (0.8-1.2in) across are borne on short stalks at the joints of the previous year's shoots, from midwinter onwards. The yellowish green flowers are purplish in the centre; the cultivar 'Luteus' is yellow without the purplish centre.

At first young bushes may not flower freely; but when growth slows down, shorter flowering wood is produced, which will flower in future years. Little pruning is needed except thinning.

Propagate by half-ripe cuttings of the current year's growth in summer, or by layering in spring.

Take care
Cut out surplus and weak shoots after flowering has finished. 41 ♦

Choisya ternata
(Mexican orange blossom)
- **Sheltered, sunny situation**
- **Not fussy over soils**
- **Spring flowering**

This handsome evergreen shrub is suitable for all except the very coldest areas. Bushes reach a height of 2-3m (6.5-10ft). The dark green glossy leaves 8-15cm (3.2-6in) long, consist of three stalkless leaflets 4-8cm (1.6-3.2in) long, tapering at either end and attached to a 3-5cm (1.2-2in) main stalk. When crushed, the foliage has a pungent smell, and the clusters of white spring flowers have a sweet fragrance. In winter the foliage is useful for floral arrangements.

Although it is hardy, often after frosts its foliage will look scorched, but as the weather improves so will the foliage. After frost damage, cut back shoots as necessary; if bushes have grown out of hand, cut hard back to old wood. For a second crop of flowers, prune back flowered shoots by about 25-30cm (10-12in) as soon as blooming has finished.

Propagate by softwood cuttings taken in summer.

Take care
Keep bushes in good shape. 41 ♦

Above: **Buddleia alternifolia**
In full bloom, this large shrub or small tree provides a superb display in the garden. Grow it in a sunny location and prune out old flowered shoots when the blooms have faded. 24▸

Left: **Berberis darwinii**
These orange-yellow flowers smother
the stems of this evergreen bush in
spring, giving way to purplish berries
during the autumn. Hardy and
densely spined, this plant is widely
grown as a garden hedge. 22♦

Right: **Buddleia globosa**
Originally from Chile and Peru, this
shrub will remain evergreen through
mild winters. The ball-like flowers
appear in early summer and are
honey-scented. Prune as required to
give the bush a good shape. 25♦

Below: **Buddleia davidii**
These highly fragrant blooms, also
available in other shades of purple,
reddish purple and in pure white,
attract butterflies during the summer
months. A popular shrub. 24♦

Above: **Camellia × williamsii 'Donation'**
Camellias thrive in soil fortified with leaf mould. In a sheltered position, this variety produces semi-double pink flowers in spring. 28♦

Left: **Calceolaria integrifolia**
Planted near a sunny wall offering some protection against frost and cold winds, this shrubby calceolaria bears clusters of the familiar pouched flowers in summer. It will grow freely after pruning in spring. 26♦

Right: **Caryopteris × clandonensis 'Kew Blue'**
This deciduous shrub also needs some protection, especially when newly planted. The dark blue flowers are produced in autumn. Prune each spring to encourage new growth. 28♦

37

Right:
Catalpa bignonioides 'Aurea'
Purple and yellow summer flowers can just be seen amidst the foliage of this attractive specimen. The large leaves – up to 25cm (10in) in length – retain their superb yellow colour throughout the season. Grow in full sun for really bright foliage. 29▶

Below right: **Ceanothus impressus**
These dense blue flowers develop freely from dark red buds during spring. In a sunny position, preferably in the protection of a wall, this evergreen shrub will form a compact bush about 1.5m (5ft) in height and width. Easily propagated from half-ripe cuttings in late summer. 30▶

Below:
Ceanothus 'Gloire de Versailles'
These impressive clusters of flowers appear during late summer and autumn. This ceanothus is deciduous and plants should be cut almost to the base each spring to encourage new flowering wood. Plant in a sunny sheltered spot in any good fertile soil, including chalky soils. 30▶

Left: **Cercis siliquastrum**
Choose a warm sunny location and a well-drained soil for this lovely Mediterranean tree; it will not thrive in damp, cold conditions. In spring the bare branches are covered with dense clusters of pink flowers. 31♦

Right:
Chimonanthes praecox 'Luteus'
These delicate sweetly scented flowers brave the cold as they appear on the bare branches of this deciduous shrub from midwinter on. Grow against a sunny wall. 32♦

Below: **Choisya ternata**
This handsome shrub provides a double bonus of glossy evergreen aromatic foliage and highly fragrant spring flowers. Prune bushes after flowering to keep them in shape. 32♦

Above:
Clerodendrum trichotomum
This autumn display of blue berries follows white spring flowers. 49♦

Below: **Cornus mas**
Bright yellow flowers cover the bare branches of this shrub or small tree as winter turns to spring. 51♦

Above: **Cornus alba 'Sibirica'**
These bright red young stems provide a striking display during the winter and early spring. Grow in full sun and hard prune in late spring for vigorous shoots the next winter. 51 ▶

Above: **Cotinus coggygria 'Notcutt's Variety'**
The deep purple foliage is the main attraction of this splendid shrub. The pink-purple flowerheads are borne more freely on poor soil. 54▶

Above: **Corylopsis spicata**
*These early spring flowers are
fragrant and freely borne on naked
branches. Protect from frost. 53♦*

Below: **Cornus stolonifera
'Flaviramea'**
*The greenish yellow stems provide
winter colour. Prune in spring. 52♦*

Above: **Cotoneaster horizontalis**
*Profuse red berries light up this hardy
and adaptable shrub during the
autumn as the glossy green leaves
turn to orange and red. Excellent on
walls, banks and as ground cover.* 54▸

Above: **Crataegus oxyacantha
'Rosea Flore Pleno'**
*Superb double pink flowers almost
smothering the new spring foliage.* 55♦

Below: **Cytisus × praecox**
*Vigorous sprays of creamy flowers
brighten this compact shrub each
spring. Grow in full sun.* 56♦

Above: **Cytisus scoparius
'Golden Sunlight'**
The rich yellow flowers of this strong *growing variety glow in the spring sunshine. Plants reach up to 2m (6.5ft) in height and width.* 56♦

Cistus 'Silver Pink'

(Rock rose)
- **Full sun**
- **Light, well-drained soil**
- **Summer flowering**

This lovely hybrid rock rose bears clear silvery pink flowers up to 7cm (2.75in) across above lance-shaped evergreen foliage. Each flower has a prominent boss of golden-yellow stamens. 'Silver Pink' is ideal for small gardens as it grows only about 75cm (30in) high. It is poor on acid soils, but perfectly hardy when grown on well-drained moderately rich soils. For a more vigorous cistus up to 2.5m (8ft) tall choose *Cistus × cyprius*. Its white flowers are enhanced by a blood-red blotch at the base of each petal.

The rose-like flowers of cistus last as a rule for only a few hours in the morning, and never more than one day, but a regular succession of buds keeps the floral display going for two or three months during fine weather. Cistus is ideal for growing on hot dry banks. The plants are hardy except in very severe winters. Propagate by half-ripe cuttings in summer.

Take care
Do not cut back into old wood.

Clerodendrum trichotomum

(Glory tree)
- **Full sun**
- **Open, fertile soil**
- **Late summer to early autumn flowering**

This deciduous species forms an open sparsely branched small tree or large bush 3-6m (10-20ft) tall. Its large oval leaves, 10-20cm (4-8in) long and 5-10cm (2-4in) wide with slightly downy stalks, are arranged oppositely on the pithy branches. Fragrant white flowers are produced at the topmost pair of leaves in late summer, followed in early autumn by a reddish five-lobed calyx; in the centre of each calyx is a bright blue pea-sized berry, which eventually changes to black. The foliage has a rubbery smell when knocked or crushed, and the pithy branches and shoots continually die back.

Flowering is improved by shortening back the previous year's growth to the last pair of buds in early spring; do this every year. Propagate by suckers or root cuttings in spring.

Take care
Do not dig, fork or hoe around these bushes, as this will encourage suckers to form – unless they are wanted for propagation. 42♦

Clethra alnifolia

(Sweet pepper bush)
- **Head in the sun, 'feet' in the shade**
- **Well-drained peaty lime-free soil**
- **Late summer flowering**

An erect hardy deciduous shrub about 2.1-2.7m (7-9ft) with a spread of 2.5-3m (8-10ft). The egg- to wedge-shaped leaves are 4-10cm (1.6-4in) long and 2-10cm (0.8-4in) wide. The fragrant creamy white flowers are borne on slender spikes that are produced on the current season's growth in the axils of the topmost leaves in late summer.

This attractive shrub is first-rate for damp sites, and thrives in industrial areas, so for those who have to garden in such areas *Clethra alnifolia* is the answer. Apart from its white aromatic flowers, its foliage gives colour in autumn.

In winter remove old stems to ground level, and thin out weak growth when the bushes become crowded. Propagate by seeds sown in peaty soil in late winter, by layering in spring or autumn, or by half-ripe cuttings taken in summer.

Take care
Keep moist at the roots.

Colutea arborescens

(Common bladder senna)
- **Sunny location**
- **Any soil, even poor and chalky soils**
- **Flowers summer to autumn**

The inflated, almost transparent, seedpods are the main attraction of this hardy deciduous shrub. The 8-15cm (3.2-6in) leaves contain nine to 13 leaflets. The yellow pea-shaped flowers are produced on the current season's growth, and each raceme bears three to seven flowers. These are followed by the seedpods; in very dry summer weather when the seedpods are very ripe, they will pop open on their own. This is the plant's method of distributing the seeds.

The hybrid *C. media* is similar in habit, also making a vigorous shrub, but the flowers are of a brown, red or coppery hue.

Bushes reach a height of about 3.6m (12ft). To keep them tidy, prune them each winter; cut back the strong young branches to within several eyes of the old wood. The flowers are borne on the current year's shoots. Propagate by seed sown in late winter, or by half-ripe heel cuttings of the current growth in late summer.

Take care
Remove unwanted seedlings.

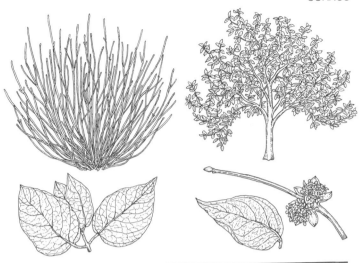

Cornus alba 'Sibirica'
(Red-barked dogwood)
- **Sun, but tolerates a little shade**
- **Any soil; damp conditions best**
- **Colourful bark and fruit**

Cornus alba is a hardy deciduous shrub that makes a thicket of erect stems. The cultivar 'Sibirica' is less rampant than the species, but the young shoots are a brighter red. The small yellowish flowers are followed by bluish pea-sized fruits. The oval leaves are opposite, fresh green above and bluish grey below. Flowers and foliage are of less importance than the richly coloured stems. Bushes reach a height of 2-2.7m (6.5-9ft) with a spread of 2.5-3m (8-10ft).

For good colour during the autumn and winter cut all stems close to the base in late spring. The result will be plenty of young stems; there will be no flowers or berries, however, but the coloured stems are the main attraction. The cultivar 'Spaethii' has golden-yellow variegated foliage, but its stems are a less brilliant red.

Propagate by hardwood cuttings in autumn, inserting them in the open ground.

Take care
Cut back every year to produce colourful stems. 43♦

Cornus mas
(Cornelian cherry)
- **Sun; will tolerate some shade**
- **Any good soil, including clay**
- **Flowers in late winter to early spring; fruit in autumn**

This deciduous large shrub or small tree grows 4.5-6m (15-20ft) tall. It is not a cherry, although in autumn it has bright red oblong fruits the size of a small plum, but with an acid flavour. In late winter to early spring, clusters of yellow flowers are produced, borne on the previous year's naked wood.

The branches spread almost to ground level, which makes it difficult to grow other plants beneath; however, if a leading shoot is selected from a young plant a main stem eventually develops, which will let the tree display its handsome bark. Normally little or no pruning is needed, apart from keeping the main trunk of a standard tree clean. Propagate by seeds sown out of doors in spring, but they may take two years to germinate.

Take care
Keep within bounds by careful pruning when necessary. 42♦

Cornus stolonifera 'Flaviramea'
- Sunny position
- Any soil; moist or wet sites
- Winter bark

Coronilla glauca
- Full sun
- Any good fertile soil, including lime or chalk
- Summer to autumn flowering

The species *C. stolonifera* is a hardy deciduous shrub, known as the Red osier dogwood. It reaches a height of 2.5m (8ft) and suckers freely by underground stems. The young shoots have purple-red bark. The leaves are dark green above and bluish grey beneath, and the white flowers in spring are followed later by white fruits.

The cultivar 'Flaviramea' grows 2-2.5m (6.5-8ft) high. The young shoots are olive to greenish yellow (some describe this dogwood as having butter-yellow bark); but when it is planted alongside a red-stemmed cultivar such as 'Sibirica' the colour combination is most striking in winter sunshine. To produce good coloured stems, cut bushes hard back each year during spring.

Propagate by hardwood cuttings about 30cm (12in) long inserted in open ground out of doors, or by suckers (both in autumn), or by layering in spring.

Take care
Provide ample moisture. 45◆

This graceful bushy evergreen shrub, a member of the pea family, grows 1.2-2m (4-6.5ft) high, or even more in favourable conditions. The bluish grey-green pinnate foliage is sometimes scorched by frost at the tips, but new growth will soon be produced. The clusters of rich yellow sweetly scented flowers stand out among the foliage.

On clay this species may flower in midwinter. It is said to be slightly tender, so choose a situation where it has some protection. A wall or fence that receives a good amount of sunshine would form an ideal backdrop for this shrub. In spring when new growth starts, tip back any dead or frosted shoots to sound live wood, and remove old or worn-out growth.

Propagate by half-ripe cuttings in early summer.

Take care
Choose a protected site for this graceful evergreen shrub.

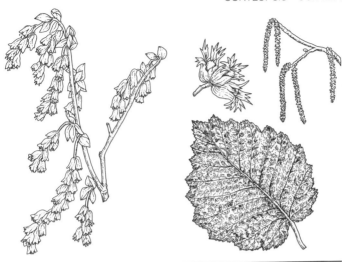

Corylopsis spicata
- **Half shade**
- **Acid or neutral fertile soil**
- **Early spring flowers; autumn foliage colour**

An attractive early-flowering deciduous hardy shrub that does best in half shade, preferably in a situation that prevents the sun shining on the bush until frost has gone, as frost can damage the flowers. It makes a bush 1.5-2.1m (5-7ft) tall and equally wide. The heart-shaped leaves, 8-10cm (3.2-4in) long and 5-8cm (2-3.2in) wide, are pale green above and bluish grey below. Drooping spikes of six to 12 yellow cowslip-scented flowers, on a 4cm (1.6in) raceme, are borne on the naked shoots of the previous year's growth in early spring. In autumn the bush displays bright yellow foliage.

As a rule no pruning is needed. Should a bush become too large for its site, it is better to prune back the shrubs around it.

Propagate by half-ripe side shoots taken with a heel during the summer. Insert them in a sand and peat mixture in a warm propagating frame.

Take care
Allow bushes to grow naturally without pruning. 45♦

Corylus maxima 'Purpurea'
(Purple-leaf filbert)
- **Sunny location**
- **Good loamy or chalk soil**
- **Summer and autumn foliage**

All species of the hazel genus are attractive deciduous shrubs grown for their foliage and catkins; the lambs'-tails are the male flowers, and the female flowers are small and red. 'Purpurea' has outstanding purple foliage, akin in colour to that of the purple beech. The toothed leaves are roundish with a heart-shaped base, 5-13cm (2-5in) long and 4-10cm (1.6-4in) wide. The male catkins are also purple. This handsome purple-leaved shrub will reach 2.5-3m (8-10ft) tall. Used as a screen it is very effective.

To obtain plenty of new growth, cut out all weaker wood during the winter, retaining the more mature, sound and healthy growth.

Propagate by rooted suckers, which can be lifted in autumn or winter and transplanted, or by layering in autumn.

Take care
Keep bushes strong by removing weak wood each year.

Cotinus coggygria 'Notcutt's Variety'

- Sunny position
- Any type of soil
- Summer flowers; spring and autumn foliage

For many years this deciduous shrub was known as *Rhus cotinus*; the species is also known as Venetian sumach. It makes a large shrub, 3.6-4.5m (12-15ft) high, with a similar width. The smoke-like inflorescences are a mixture of pink and purple. The striking purple foliage, which when it first unfolds in spring is a shade of crimson, later becomes a rich purple, and finally is semi-translucent.

This shrub does not need a rich soil, and indeed flowers more freely on a poor one. The leaves are oval, slightly notched at the apex, and 4-8cm (1.6-3.2in) long. Provided only foliage is wanted, prune annually in spring; cut down young wood, but not too severely, just before new growth starts. If you want the smoke-like flowers, however, avoid pruning except to keep the bush in good shape.

Propagate by half-ripe cuttings of the current year's wood, in mid- to late summer.

Take care
Prune for foliage, not for flowers. 44♦

Cotoneaster horizontalis

(Herringbone or Fishbone cotoneaster)

- Sun or partial shade
- Any good soil, including chalk
- Spring flowers; autumn colour

This low-growing deciduous cotoneaster gets its common names because the bare horizontal branches look rather like the bones of a fish. It has dark glossy green leaves above, mostly smooth beneath through sometimes with a few scattered hairs; the leaves are 6-12mm (0.25-0.5in) long, and 2cm (0.8in) wide. In spring the white flowers suffused with pink are a great attraction to bees seeking nectar. In autumn there are bright red berries, and the dark green foliage changes to shades of orange and red before it finally falls. This is an excellent low-growing shrub for ground cover or to clothe banks. Bushes reach a height of 60-90cm (24-36in). The cultivar 'Variegatus' has leaves attractively edged with white.

Propagate by seed which should be stratified (stored damp to soften the seed coat) and sown in spring, or by half-ripe cuttings in summer or hardwood cuttings in autumn.

Take care
Cut out dead shoots in late winter. 46♦

Crataegus × lavallei

(Hawthorn)
- **Sunny position**
- **Any good soil, including chalk**
- **Summer flowering**

Crataegus × lavallei is a sturdy upright tree reaching a height of 4.5-6m (15-20ft). The large oval leaves are 4-10cm (1.6-4in) long and 2.5-6.5cm (1-2.5in) wide, dark and glossy with a leathery texture. The foliage will hang on well into winter. In late spring to early summer it produces flat-topped clusters of white flowers, each 2.5cm (1in) in diameter. These are followed in autumn by large orange-red berries, speckled with brown dots; the berries last throughout the winter and show up well against the dark green foliage, which later turns a bronzy red before finally falling.

The heads of standard trees may become crowded, but they should not be thinned, as this will spoil their natural shape.

Propagate by stratified seed; sow it out of doors, about 18 months after gathering.

Take care
Stake young trees if they are planted where wind could move them and injure the root system.

Crataegus oxyacantha

(Hawthorn)
- **Sunny location**
- **Any good soil, including chalk**
- **Spring flowering**

This is the common hawthorn or may. The leaves are mostly oval, wedge-shaped at the base, with three to five lobes, rounded or slightly pointed, and dark glossy green. The flowers, 2cm (0.8in) wide, are produced in flat-topped clusters of six to 12 flowers.

The cultivars worthy of mention are 'Paul's Scarlet' and 'Rosea Flore Pleno', both double-flowered and without berries. 'Paul's Scarlet' has double scarlet flowers; it makes a rounded, bushy head, about 6-7.6m (20-25ft) tall and as wide. 'Rosea Flore Pleno' is similar to 'Paul's Scarlet', except that it has double pink flowers. Both trees are superb for a small garden. By careful pruning after flowering has finished they can be kept within bounds.

Propagate by budding or grafting onto stocks of *C. oxyacantha* in spring.

Take care
Stake securely after planting, until well established. 47♦

55

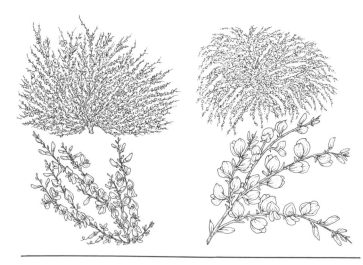

Cytisus × praecox

(Warminster broom)
- **Sunny location**
- **Any good soil**
- **Spring flowering**

This free-flowering broom of a dense rounded habit reaches a height about 1-1.5m (3.3-5ft). It produces arching sprays packed with masses of beautiful creamy-yellow flowers in spring. Its simple grey-green single leaves are about 1cm (0.4in) long, and borne on silky shoots. The shrub's only fault is that it has a slightly disagreeable odour when in flower.

Warminster broom sets good fertile seed, but does not come true from seed; nevertheless, worthwhile varieties have been raised. One of Dutch origin, 'Allgold', bears deep yellow flowers on slightly taller bushes. Another raised in Germany, called 'Golden Spear', has bright golden-yellow flowers and is of a more compact habit. Both these varieties remain in flower for almost a month.

Propagate by seed sown out of doors in spring, or by heel or nodal cuttings during the summer.

Take care
Do not cut into old wood; trim young shoots only lightly. 47♦

Cytisus scoparius

(Broom)
- **Full sun**
- **Any good deep soil, but avoid chalky soils**
- **Spring flowering**

The common broom is a free-flowering deciduous shrub, but when the foliage has fallen the green stems give an evergreen appearance. The shrub reaches a height of 1.5-2m (5-6.5ft) and as much in width.

The hybrids prefer a deep soil, neutral or slightly acid, but not poor shallow soils. They like plenty of sun. The variety 'Golden Sunlight' grows 60cm (24in) high and 90cm (36in) wide; above the dark, dull green foliage, orange-yellow flowers (singly or in pairs) appear on 30-45cm (12-18in) inflorescences in spring. The many varieties also include the yellow and crimson flowered 'Andreanus'; the cream and yellow 'Cornish Cream'; and the lovely 1.5m (5ft) 'Burkwoodii' in shades of maroon, purple and red.

The only pruning required is to cut off roughly two-thirds of the previous year's shoots.

Propagate by seed sown out of doors in spring, or by heel or nodal cuttings during summer.

Take care
Do not cut into old wood. 48♦

Daphne × burkwoodii 'Somerset'

- **Full sunshine**
- **A well-drained moist soil**
- **Flowers late spring to early summer**

The semi-evergreen or almost deciduous shrub 'Somerset' is a clone of *D. × burkwoodii*. It reaches about 1m (39in) in height and makes a sparingly branched bush with 2.5cm (1in) almost lance-shaped leaves. This clone has sweetly scented blush-pink tubular flowers, the outside flushed with rose, and produced in bunches of six on short lateral shoots.

Like most daphnes 'Somerset' likes good drainage, yet it must have an ample supply of moisture. Dryness at the roots must be avoided if the shrub is to thrive in the garden. 'Somerset' does well on a sandy loam.

As daphnes transplant badly, always obtain young container grown plants, which should be planted in their permanent positions as soon as possible. Propagate by half-ripe cuttings during the summer.

Take care
Prevent dryness at the roots. 65♦

Daphne mezereum

(Mezereon)
- **Sun, but tolerates some shade**
- **Any good fertile soil**
- **Flowers late winter or early spring**

When *Daphne mezereum* blooms in late winter, it tells us that spring is just around the corner. This colourful and fragrant deciduous shrub reaches a height of 1-1.5m (3.3-5ft) and as much in width. Spear-like leaves taper at the base and are either pointed or rounded at the apex; they are 4-9cm (1.6-3.5in) long and 6-20mm (0.25-0.8in) wide. The sweetly scented purplish red flowers are produced in twos and threes on erect naked wood. The green berries later become bright red, and these are attractive to blackbirds.

As this is not a long-lived shrub, have a few seedlings or plants from cuttings available in case of losses. Usually a few berries drop to the ground, and some will germinate. Propagate by seed when it is ripe, or by taking nearly ripe cuttings in early autumn. Usually no pruning is needed, but if a shoot needs cutting to improve the shape of the bush, do this in spring.

Take care
Be sure to have young plants available as replacements. 66♦

Daphne odora 'Aureomarginata'

- Full sun
- Any well-drained soil
- Flowers late winter/early spring

This evergreen shrub has a delicious fragrance. The cultivar 'Aureomarginata' is hardier and more vigorous than the species. Even so, in cold areas choose a sheltered position; otherwise any good open site will suffice. It can be grown successfully in a well-drained clay soil and where there is chalk in the soil, although it does not need it.

The narrow oval leaves, 4-9cm (1.6-3.5in) long, are faintly margined in creamy white. The flowers, reddish purple on the outside and paler within, are sweetly scented; one plant will scent the entire garden in late winter and early spring. This shrub will grow to 1.2-1.8m (4-6ft) tall, and about the same in width.

Propagate by layering or by taking half-ripe cuttings of the current year's growth during midsummer.

Take care
Prune after flowering, but only when really necessary. 67♦

Deutzia × elegantissima 'Fasciculata'

- Sunny situation
- Good loamy soil; tolerates lime
- Spring flowering

Deutzias are deciduous shrubs, with panicles of dainty flowers in spring. They need ample moisture and good loamy soil; the majority tolerate lime. 'Fasciculata' makes a graceful shrub up to 1.5m (5ft) tall. Deutzias are wiry shrubs, and their oval-shaped foliage is rather wrinkled. The flowers are borne on the previous year's growth; they are almost 2.5cm (1in) wide, bright rosy pink on the outside and paler within. Another equally beautiful deutzia is 'Rosalind', which has deep carmine flowers.

Every two years, thin out old flowering shoots and any dead branches. Although deutzias are winter-hardy, they make rather early growth, and in frost pockets or low-lying districts they can become frosted.

Propagate by half-ripe cuttings inserted where there is gentle bottom heat during early to mid-summer, or by hardwood cuttings inserted out of doors in autumn.

Take care
Provide ample moisture. 67♦

Elaeagnus pungens 'Maculata'

- Full sunlight
- Any soil, including chalk
- Year-round foliage

The cultivar 'Maculata' is an evergreen spreading shrub which can reach 2.7-3.6m (9-12ft) high and 3-4.5m (10-15ft) wide. The striking foliage is marked with a rich yellow patch in the centre of each leaf. The leaves are often as much as 11.5cm (4.5in) long by 6.5cm (2.5in) wide. The foliage lights up any part of the garden, especially when backed by dark evergreen shrubs, such as *Prunus lusitanica* (Portugal laurel) or *Buxus sempervirens* (Box). This shrub has also been known as *E.p. aureo-variegata*.

From time to time green shoots may appear; when this happens, such shoots must be cut out to preserve the variegated foliage.

Propagate by half-ripe cuttings inserted in gentle heat during midsummer, or by hardwood cuttings taken in late autumn.

Take care
Remove any green shoots as soon as they are noticed.

Embothrium coccineum

(Fire bush)

- Shade
- Moist loamy lime-free soil
- Flowers in spring and early summer

This showy evergreen shrub or small tree is sometimes, though rarely, semi-deciduous. It must have a cool root run, which can be achieved where there is a moist loamy soil free of lime or chalk. Also it must have shelter from cold drying winds. Provided it has shelter, and a modicum of shade from surrounding trees, it should eventually give a spectacular display of brilliant orange-scarlet flowers in spring and early summer. The dark glossy green leaves are greyish green above and paler beneath. As a bush it will reach a height of 3.6-4.5m (12-15ft), and as a tree 7.6-9m (25-30ft) high. No pruning is necessary.

Propagate by seeds sown in late winter under glass, or by root cuttings taken in winter and inserted in small pots where there is moderate bottom heat.

Take care
Choose a sheltered situation, as trees are not very deep-rooted. 69▸

Enkianthus campanulatus

- **Full sun**
- **Moist loamy lime-free soil**
- **Spring flowers; autumn foliage**

When young this hardy deciduous shrub has a slightly erect habit, but as it develops it becomes a densely branched bushy shrub, which normally requires no pruning. It can reach a height of 1.5-2.7m (5-9ft) and almost as much in width. The finely toothed dull green leaves are 2.5-6.5cm (1-2.5in) long and 1.2-3.5cm (0.5-1.4in) wide. The bell-shaped creamy yellow pendulous flowers, veined and red-tipped, form pretty clusters, each flower on an 8mm (0.3in) stalk. The flowers are produced in spring on the terminal buds of the previous year's shoots. In autumn, the foliage changes to attractive shades of yellow and red.

Enkianthus needs a cool moist peaty soil. When bushes become overgrown or misshapen, cut them hard back. Provided new growth appears from the base, all is well.

Propagate by seed under glass in late winter, by softwood cuttings in summer, or by layering in spring.

Take care
Note whether plenty of new growth is appearing from the base. 68♦

Erica cineria
(Bell heather; Scotch heath; Grey Heath)

- **Full sun**
- **Lime-free or neutral soil**
- **Summer to autumn flowers**

Apart from the names mentioned above, this attractive species is also sometimes known as Five-leaved heath or Twisted heath. It is an easy plant to grow, and loves to be in the sun, with a cool root run; it will tolerate a hot dry position. Like other ericas it likes peat, but always use a mixture of peat and medium loam; and avoid rich soils. General care is as for *E. herbacea*, except that it must have a lime-free or neutral soil.

Cultivars vary in height from 10cm to 30cm (4-12in), and a few are 45-75cm (18-30in) tall. 'Lady Skelton' is 15cm (6in) high, with deep crimson flowers above dark green foliage in summer; it makes a neat dwarf plant, but is a rather slow grower. For later flowering, choose 'New Salmon', with long spikes of salmon pink flowers 45cm (18in) tall. Trim off faded blooms after flowering has finished.

Propagate by heel or nodal cuttings in late summer, or by layering in spring.

Take care
Make sure peat is properly moistened before use. 68♦

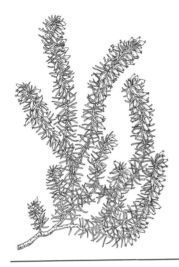 

Erica herbacea
(syn. E. carnea)
(Winter heath; Snow heath)
- **Open sunny situation**
- **Light soil; tolerates lime**
- **Autumn to spring flowers**

This attractive species was known as *Erica carnea*, but it is now *Erica herbacea*. There is a wide variety of colours, from white, pink, red, and rosy purple to dark carmine red. The cultivar 'December Red', 15-23cm (6-9in) high, has bright rose-pink flowers above a mat of dark green leaves from early winter. 'Springwood White' is the same height with light green foliage and long white spikes.

Choose an open situation and avoid rich soils. Plant deeply, ie, with the lowest foliage resting on the soil, in early spring. The tufted shrubs produce tight hummocks 15-30cm (6-12in) high, forming prostrate spreading plants. The small dark glossy green foliage is usually arranged in whorls of four. Flowers are produced singly or in pairs, in the leaf axils of the previous year's growth. With shears trim all faded blooms after flowering has finished.

Propagate by heel or nodal cuttings in late summer, or by layering in spring.

Take care
Moisten peat before use. 71♦

Escallonia
- **Sun loving**
- **Well-drained soil; tolerates lime**
- **Summer flowering**

The evergreen escallonias are not considered 100% hardy. In particularly cold areas they go to 'sleep' earlier and 'wake up' later than those in warmer regions, where they flower up to midwinter and then are frosted in late winter.

The following two hybrids are especially recommended. E. 'Apple Blossom' is a slow-growing variety with pink and white flowers; it reaches a height of 1.5-2m (5-6.5ft). E. 'C.F. Ball' is a free flowering strong-growing escallonia, with large red flowers from summer to early autumn; it reaches 2.1-2.5m (7-8ft) in favoured localities.

Both these escallonias do well by the sea, as they all do. No regular pruning is required; cut back occasionally after flowering to keep bushes shapely, or do it in spring. Escallonias flower on one-year-old wood.

Propagate by half-ripe cuttings during summer, or by seed sown in late winter under glass.

Take care
The soil must not be too rich. 70♦

Eucryphia glutinosa

- **Sunny location; roots in shade**
- **Cool lime free moist soil**
- **Late summer flowering**

This hardy deciduous or partially evergreen small tree-like shrub has an erect shapely branching habit. It has clusters of pinnate opposite leaves consisting of three or five oval leaflets, 4-6.5cm (1.6-2.5in) long. The flowers, produced either singly or in pairs, each have four petals 6.5cm (2.5in) across, with a central boss of yellow anthers. The pure white flowers are borne in the leaf axils at the end of the shoot.

This is not the easiest of shrubs to establish, propagate, or transplant. Provide it wih moist peaty soil, free of lime or chalk, and keep its roots shaded. Do not prune.

Propagate by half-ripe cuttings of side shoots taken with a heel during summer, or by layering in late summer. Whichever is tried, be prepared for losses.

Take care
Allow eucryphias to grow naturally as they resent pruning or training. Remove overhanging branches from nearby trees before their shape is affected. 71◆

Eucryphia × nymansensis 'Nymansay'

- **Sheltered sunny position**
- **Cool moist soil**
- **Late summer flowering**

'Nymansay' is a natural hybrid between *E. glutinosa* and *E. cordifolia*. It eventually grows to a height of 9-12m (30-39ft) with a spread of 3.6-4.5m (12-15ft) but will take several years to reach such dimensions. It needs shelter from cold winds. The evergreen toothed leaves are mostly trifoliate; the largest and central leaf is 8cm (3.2in) long and 3.5cm (1.4in) wide. The leaves are glossy green above and paler beneath. This eucryphia has large white flowers from late summer to early autumn, with four or five petals, and a large boss of thin stamens crowned by pink anthers; each flower is 6-9cm (2.3-3.5in) across.

No pruning is needed; allow the tree to develop naturally. It is a robust grower. Propagate by half-ripe cuttings of side shoots taken with a heel during summer, or by layering in late summer. Be prepared for losses.

Take care
Remove overhanging tree branches before they cause damage. 73◆

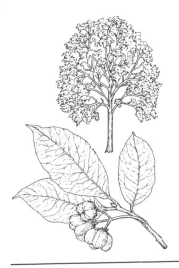

Euonymus europaeus 'Red Cascade'

(Spindle-tree)
- **Full sun**
- **Any ordinary soil**
- **Flowers early summer, fruit and foliage in autumn**

The cultivar 'Red Cascade' is one of the most striking shrubs in autumn. The yellowish green flowers are insignificant in early summer; but in autumn, the ripe 2cm (0.8in) fruits display four rosy-red lobes, which open to show large orange seeds among the scarlet foliage. It forms a bush or small tree 2-2.7m (6.5-9ft) high and as wide.

To have a good crop of fruit it needs a pollinator such as *E. latifolius*, which also has brilliant autumn foliage, and larger scarlet fruits than *E. europaeus*. Watch for caterpillar damage during the flowering season; they feed on the oval-shaped leaves. To prevent this, spray with trichlorphon or malathion, which will also deal with attacks of blackfly. No regular pruning is needed, though occasional thinning may be necessary to keep the bush shapely; do this in spring.

Propagate by seeds sown in spring under glass, or by hardwood cuttings taken with a heel in autumn.

Take care
Deal with blackfly or caterpillars.

Exochorda racemosa

(Pearl Bush)
- **Sunny situation**
- **Fairly rich acid soil; dislikes lime**
- **Spring flowering**

This is a deciduous bushy shrub that grows to a height of 3m (10ft). Pure white flowers, 3.5-4cm (1.4-1.6in) across, are produced in spring, on erect racemes 8-10cm (3.2-4in) long on short twigs of the previous year's growth. Each branch can carry sprays of the snow-white flowers up to 30-45cm (12-18in) long and as much as 20-25cm (8-10in) wide, their weight often making the branches bend.

To obtain such a fine display, bushes should be thinned out. As soon as the flowers are over, young shoots should also be reduced by removing those that are very thin or weak, especially if the bush is overcrowded. It may also be necessary to remove developing shoots in spring when they have produced three to four leaves.

Propagate by softwood cuttings taken with a heel after midsummer. In autumn it may be possible to remove a rooted sucker growth.

Take care
Plant in good rich soil.

Fatsia japonica

- Sun or semi-shade
- Good loamy soil
- Flowers autumn to early winter

This magnificent hardy evergreen shrub has enormous palmate foliage. It makes a large spreading shrub or small tree up to 4.5m (15ft) high, and equally wide. The leathery dark green glossy leaves, of seven to nine lobes, are 30-40cm (12-16in) across, attached to a heart-shaped base and a stalk 30cm (12in) or more long. In late autumn to early winter this shrub produces large clusters of milky-white flowers, which form globose heads at the end of the shoots; these are followed by black fruits.

Fatsia is an ideal shrub to grow in coastal areas and in industrial cities. For many years this evergreen was considered a greenhouse shrub; fortunately it was eventually realized that it is hardy.

When *F. japonica* is allowed to grow naturally, it may be necessary to restrict its growth; do this in spring when branches can be cut down to ground level. Propagate by half-ripe cuttings in late summer, inserting them singly in small pots in a propagator with bottom heat.

Take care
Plant in a sheltered position. 72♦

Forsythia intermedia 'Spectabilis'

- Full sun
- Any good soil, even chalk
- Spring flowering

This hardy deciduous shrub, 2.5-3m (8-10ft) tall and almost as wide, is known to most gardeners for its colourful display in spring. The bright yellow flowers are borne singly or in twos and threes in the axils of the broad lance-shaped leaves. 'Spectabilis' has large rich yellow flowers. The recent 'Lynwood' has even larger broad-petalled flowers.

Forsythias do not seem to mind how much they are pruned, but if cut hard back every year they will not produce many flowers. New shoots, made after the flowers have faded, will bud up during the year and flower the following spring. Each year cut out a few of the oldest growths to encourage new wood from the base; if this is not done, a mass of twiggy growth accumulates in the centre of a bush, which causes non- or poor flowering wood. Cut newly planted bushes back to within 30cm (12in) of ground level.

Propagate by softwood cuttings in summer with heat, or take hardwood cuttings in autumn.

Take care
Cut old growth after flowering. 72-3♦

Above:
Daphne × burkwoodii 'Somerset'
In a moist but well-drained soil this
semi-evergreen shrub is covered with
fragrant blush-pink blooms during
spring and early summer. 57♦

Above: **Daphne mezereum**
*These scented flower clusters are
produced in very early spring on the
bare branches. They are replaced in
summer and autumn by green berries
that gradually turn bright red.* 57♦

Above: **Daphne odora 'Aureomarginata'**
Highly fragrant flowers borne amidst attractive evergreen foliage. 58♦

Below: **Deutzia × elegantissima 'Fasciculata'**
An easy-care deciduous shrub grown for these dainty spring flowers. 58♦

Above: **Enkianthus campanulatus**
These bell-shaped flowers adorn the shrub in spring. The autumn foliage turns bright yellow and red. 60♦

Below: **Erica cinerea 'Lady Skelton'**
A summer-flowering heather with deep crimson blooms. An excellent ground cover for lime-free soils. 60♦

Above: **Embothrium coccineum**
*These splendid fiery flowers are
produced during the spring and early
summer. This evergreen bush or
small tree needs shelter from cold
winds and a lime-free soil. 59▸*

Above: **Escallonia 'Apple Blossom'**
The glossy evergreen leaves and
delicate pink-and-white flowers make
a fine display in summer. Grow in the
shelter of a wall in cold areas.
Excellent for seaside gardens. 61◗

Above: **Erica herbacea 'December Red'**
An attractive winter-flowering heath for open spots and light soils. 61♦

Below: **Eucryphia glutinosa**
These superb blooms appear in late summer. Needs a sunny protected site and cool moist lime-free soil. 62♦

Left: **Fatsia japonica**
Newly emerging leaves and black fruits adorn this plant in spring. The white flowers are produced in autumn. Grown for its handsome palmate foliage, this shrub thrives particularly well near the sea. 64▶

Right: **Eucryphia × nymansensis 'Nymansay'**
These late-summer flowers are up to 9cm (3.5in) across. This fine hybrid is said to tolerate lime in the soil and needs a protected site to thrive. 62▶

Below: **Forsythia intermedia 'Spectabilis'**
In spring the emerging leaves of this deciduous shrub are joined by bright yellow flowers that provide welcome colour in the garden. Prune carefully to encourage bloom. 64▶

Above: **Garrya elliptica**
In the protection of a sunny wall, the male plant of this evergreen shrub puts on a striking show of long catkins in late winter. Thrives in moist well-drained soil that is not too rich. 82♦

Above: **Gaultheria shallon**
*An excellent evergreen shrub for
ground cover in lime-free soils. Lovely
flowers in early summer. 82♦*

Below: **Fuchsia 'Mrs Popple'**
*A superb hardy hybrid for summer
colour. Provide a cool root run but
plenty of sun. Prune in spring. 81♦*

Above: **Genista lydia**
This crop of bright yellow flowers appears in early summer. The plant spreads freely in hummocks about 80cm (32in) high and enjoys a sunny situation on well-drained, fairly poor soils. Protect from frost. 83♦

Left: **Genista hispanica**
To ensure a good display of early summer flowers, grow this fine shrub on a poor well-drained soil; rich soils produce soft growth vulnerable to damage caused by frost. 83♦

Right: **Hamamelis mollis**
These curious spidery flowers are produced through the winter months. They are fragrant and flowering shoots can be cut for indoor decoration. Grow in well-drained neutral or slightly acid soils. 84♦

Above: **Helianthemum 'Rhodanthe Carneum'**
The silver-grey foliage acts as the perfect foil for these bright pink and orange summer flowers. An ideal plant for dry sunny banks. 85♦

Right: **Hypericum 'Hidcote'**
This shrub is difficult to beat for dependable colour from midsummer until autumn. The golden flowers are up to 8cm (3.2in) across. Prune each spring for vigorous bloom. 89♦

Below:
Hibiscus syriacus 'Woodbridge'
These magnificent rich pink flowers are produced from late summer until early autumn. This deciduous shrub thrives in full sun and dry soil. 86♦

Above: **Kalmia latifolia**
Beautiful in bloom and handsome in leaf, this evergreen shrub thrives in moist lime-free soils. 89♦

Below: **Hydrangea 'Blue Wave'**
This vigorous Lacecap hydrangea provides shades of pink and blue throughout the summer months. 87♦

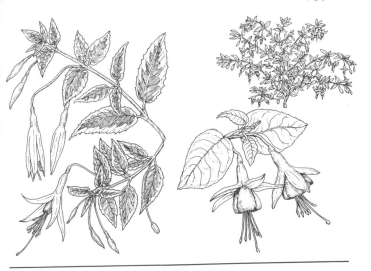

Fuchsia magellanica

- **Full sun; roots cool**
- **Most soils, including lime and chalk**
- **Summer flowering**

This hardy deciduous shrub has flowers with a red tube and a purple corolla. Plants reach a height of 2.5m (8ft). The species has leaves up to 2.5cm (1in) long. The beautiful variety 'Gracilis' has slender arching branches and small scarlet and violet flowers, and is very free-blooming. 'Variegata' has green leaves strikingly marked with margins of creamy-white flushed with pink, which set off the dainty scarlet and purple flowers.

'Versicolor' has slender stems, and its silvery grey-green leaves are margined with creamy-white stripes; the young leaves are rose-tinted, with the variegated portions bright red. To develop the beautiful foliage, this fuchsia must have full sun. These hardy fuchsias will thrive in most soils, provided they are deep and enriched with peat or compost. The plants need a cool root run but can occupy a sunny corner in the garden. For full cultivation and propagation details see Fuchsia 'Mrs. Popple'.

Take care
Plant deeply and protect the base in cold winters.

Fuchsia 'Mrs. Popple'

- **Full sun; roots cool**
- **Most soils, including lime and chalk**
- **Summer flowering**

Fuchsias are herbaceous or shrubby plants and some varieties including 'Mrs. Popple' are hardy. 'Mrs. Popple' has single blooms with scarlet tubes and sepals and deep violet corollas.

Fuchsias are not fussy over soil, but this should be prepared by double digging. Incorporate large quantities of peat moistened before use, well-rotted farmyard manure, leaf-mould or wood ash. Fuchsia roots appreciate a cool root run. Plant in late spring or early summer. When planting, place the top of the ball of soil 8cm (3.2in) below ground level, as a precaution against frosts. In early spring prune back almost to soil level; at the same time apply fertilizer and a dressing of well-rotted manure. In early summer give another application of fertilizer, and yet another during the summer. In the first year, water until established.

Propagate by softwood cuttings in early spring in a greenhouse at 16°C (60°F). Take cuttings below a node, ie where leaves join the stem.

Take care
Protect base in cold areas. 75♦

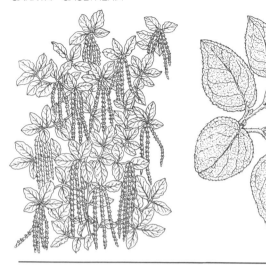

Garrya elliptica

- **Sunny location**
- **Ordinary soil, but moisture-holding**
- **Catkins early to late winter**

A striking evergreen catkin-bearing shrub that thrives in the protection of a wall where it can receive good light. In favoured areas, bushes reach as much as 5m (16.4ft) tall. The oval wavy-margined leathery leaves, 4-8cm (1.6-3.2in) long, are matt grey-green above and woolly underneath. In winter the bush has attractive pendent greyish-green male catkins 15-25cm (6-10in) long; when brushed or shaken a shower of soft yellowish green pollen is produced.

This shrub does not require a rich soil, but should have plenty of sun and moisture. Choose pot-grown plants, as it is not a good transplanter, so small plants are preferable to large ones. Little or no pruning is needed.

Propagate by seeds sown in spring in a cool greenhouse. For male plants grafting is necessary during late winter under glass in heat. Layering is possible in summer.

Take care
Do not be too generous with manure, but do not allow plants to become dry at the roots. 74♦

Gaultheria shallon

(Salal; Shallon)
- **Sun or shade**
- **Lime-free peaty acid soils**
- **Flowers in late spring to early summer, fruits in autumn**

This useful hardy evergreen shrub forms a dense thicket, sending up many stems from the base; it reaches a height of 71cm-2m (28in-6.5ft). It spreads by underground stems. The young reddish bristly branches later become rough with age. The leathery dark green leaves are attached to reddish hairy stalks. The pinkish white egg-shaped flowers are produced in late spring to early summer, and followed in late summer and autumn by dark purple berries.

This is an ideal shrub where a dense evergreen thicket or ground cover is needed in moist, shady areas. As a rule little pruning is needed except cutting out dead stems or reducing live ones with secateurs. If it becomes too dense, chunks can be cut out with a sharp spade.

Propagate by division in spring, by seeds sown under glass in late winter or out of doors in early spring, or by layering in autumn.

Take care
Do not let this species overrun any precious shrubs nearby. 75♦

Genista hispanica

(Spanish gorse)
- **Sunny position**
- **Well-drained ordinary soil**
- **Flowers in late spring and early summer**

A deciduous shrub, up to 80cm (32in) high and 2.5m (8ft) wide, with an almost evergreen appearance because of the deep green of its dense tangle of twigs and spines. Mounds of this delightful ground-hugging shrub become a cushion of pea-shaped, golden-yellow flowers in late spring and early summer.

This gorse does not like rich heavily manured soil; if given such liberal treatment, plants become soft and growth will be rank. As a result, winter frosts will damage them and spoil the next season's flowers.

Pruning consists of a light clipping as soon as flowering is over. If bushes are damaged by frost, remove all dead wood. Peg down living growth, covering it with leaf-mould, to encourage rooting of the base stems.

Propagate by seeds sown out of doors in early spring, or by heel cuttings in summer.

Genista lydia
- **Full sun**
- **Well-drained soil; tolerates lime**
- **Flowers in late spring to early summer**

This hummock-forming deciduous shrub will reach a height of 80cm (32in). The bright golden-yellow flowers are produced usually in clusters of four at the end of leafy twigs on pendulous green five-angled branches during late spring and early summer.

It will tolerate lime, but this is by no means essential. What it does need is a well-drained, sunny position. Although hardy, plants may succumb after a mild wet autumn followed by early winter frosts or late spring frosts; when this happens, scrap the plant and start afresh. Where more compact plants are needed, light pruning can be given as soon as the flowers fade.

Propagate by seeds sown under glass in late winter or out of doors in early spring. Heel cuttings can be taken during the summer.

Take care
Do not give this shrub too much manure or fertilizer. 76♦

Take care
Choose a well-drained place protected from draughts. 76-7♦

Griselina littoralis

- Sun; tolerates slight shade
- Any good fertile soil
- All year evergreen foliage

This handsome evergreen shrub or tree has flattish stems with large glossy leaves, dark apple green above and paler green beneath; they are oval and leathery, 4-10cm (1.6-4in) long and 6.5cm (2.5in) wide, blunt at the apex and unequally sided at the base, on yellowish stalks. The small, yellowish green flowers produced in spring are insignificant among the striking foliage.

This evergreen shrub is a first-rate subject for coastal gardens and can be grown as a large bush or small tree. Bushes can easily be maintained at 2.5-3m (8-10ft), or small trees 6-14m (20-46ft) high. Little or no pruning is needed, though sometimes extra long growths require shortening to keep bushes shapely; this can be done between spring and summer.

Propagate by hardwood cuttings in autumn, from side shoots with a small heel attached.

Take care
Carefully cut back any shoots that are damaged by winter frosts.

Hamamelis mollis

(Chinese witch hazel)
- Sunny position
- Good fertile soil, but not alkaline
- Winter flowering

An elegant deciduous shrub or small tree that may reach 5.5m (18ft) tall, with a spread of 4.5m (15ft). Its zigzag branches are downy, especially when young. The oval leaves, slightly rough above and hairy beneath are borne on short stalks. After flowering the foliage is a dull green, changing to yellow in autumn. In winter, curious spider-like fragrant golden-yellow flowers are produced in clusters on the bare twigs of the previous summer's growth. 'Pallida' has sulphur-yellow flowers, and beautiful yellow autumn foliage.

The flowers seem resistant to the vagaries of cold winters, and it is often possible to have a few sprays in the house in midwinter. Pruning can take place when short stems are cut for indoor decoration; unwanted long branches can be reduced in early spring.

Propagation by grafting in spring, or by layering in early spring.

Take care
Allow bushes to grow naturally. 77

Hebe 'Midsummer Beauty'

- **Full sun**
- **Any good fertile and alkaline soil**
- **Flowers from early summer to early winter**

At one time, all hebes were generally included in the genus *Veronica*; but now botanists refer to all the evergreen shrubby types as *hebes*, and all the herbaceous perennials as *veronicas*. 'Midsummer Beauty' is a hardy free-flowering evergreen shrub reaching 1.2m (4ft) tall and 1.5-2.1m (5-7ft) wide. The glossy green lance-like leaves, up to 10cm (4in) long and 3.5cm (1.4in) wide, are reddish purple when young, especially on the midrib. The young shoots are light green, becoming greeny brown when older. It has 15-20cm (6-8in) racemes of lavender-purple flowers with a slight fragrance, from early summer to early winter.

No regular pruning is needed; remove old flowers and thin any crowded bushes in autumn. If severe pruning is required, do this in spring.

Propagate by half-ripe cuttings in late summer or early autumn.

Take care
Keep bushes well shaped by careful pruning when necessary.

Helianthemum 'Rhodanthe Carneum'

(Sun rose; Rock rose)
- **Full sun**
- **Any good garden soil**
- **Flowering late spring to just after midsummer**

The hybrid 'Rhodanthe Carneum' has soft wild-rose pink flowers with an orange-yellow centre, and silver-grey foliage. It makes a fine clump 23-30cm (9-12in) high, and will spread to as much as 80cm (32in) across. 'Henfield Brilliant' has glistening brick-red flowers that cover a humock of silver-green foliage, silvery beneath; its dimensions are the same as those of 'Rhodanthe Carneum'. 'Wisley Pink' has pale pink flowers with an orange-yellow centre, and grey foliage.

The only pruning needed is to cut off old flowerheads and shorten long straggly shoots; from time to time it may be necessary to give the whole plant a trim over with a pair of secateurs.

Propagate during mid- to late summer by half-ripe cuttings, with or without a heel, inserted in a cold frame.

Take care
Keep plants healthy by careful trimming when needed. 78◆

85

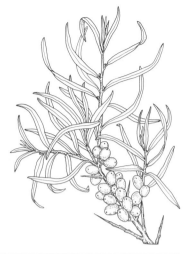

Hibiscus syriacus 'Woodbridge'
(Shrubby mallow)
- **Full sun**
- **Any good well-drained soil**
- **Flowers summer to autumn**

This hibiscus is a hardy deciduous flowering shrub with a stiff, erect growing habit. The stems are greyish white and bear smooth, coarsely toothed green leaves up to 10cm (4in) long. The large trumpet-shaped flowers are 6.5-10cm (2.5-4in) across, with a distinctive yellow stamial column (like an erect clapper in a bell). The flowers are produced singly on short stalks in the axils of the leaves. 'Woodbridge' has deep rose to rich pink flowers, blotched with carmine at the base of the petals; the single flowers are 10cm (4in) across.

For hibiscus to flourish they like hot dry soil and full sun. In a hot dry summer and autumn they are in their element. Little pruning is necessary apart from cutting out dead wood during spring or summer, and shortening the young shoots to keep bushes well balanced.

Propagate by taking half-ripe cuttings of short side shoots with a slight heel during the summer.

Take care
Avoid damp situations. 78

Hippophae rhamnoides
(Sea buckthorn)
- **Sunny location**
- **Any ordinary or alkaline soil**
- **Spring flowers; autumn fruit**

This is a hardy deciduous shrub, and sometimes a tree. It will reach a height of 3-6m (10-20ft) and almost as wide. Its narrow leaves, almost stalkless, are dark greyish green above and silvery grey beneath. The small solitary flowers produced in spring are followed in early autumn by clusters of egg-shaped orange-coloured fruits smothering the greyish brown stems. As the berries contain an acid yellow juice, they are not a favourite food for the birds.

This is a dioecious shrub, with the male and female flowers on separate plants. To get a good crop of berries, grow six females to one male, or in a very small garden three to one. It is not fussy over soil, and is an ideal shrub for seaside areas. Little or no pruning is needed.

Propagate by layering in autumn, or by seeds stored in dry sand through the winter and sown out of doors in spring, or by suckers.

Take care
Plant one male shrub to several females for abundant berries.

Hydrangea macrophylla

Hortensia group
- **Sun or light shade**
- **A neutral or slightly acid soil**
- **Flowers summer to autumn**

The Hortensia hydrangeas are those seen in gardens and florists' shops during late summer and early autumn. They have large globose heads, unlike the flat-headed Lacecaps. Dwarf varieties may reach a height of 45cm (18in), and tall ones 1.5m (5ft). The pink and red varieties give an extra display in autumn, when the blooms take on brilliant red and scarlet colourings, lasting well into the frosty seasons.

Blue varieties thrive and colour more freely in very acid soil; they are helped by adding aluminium sulphate to the soil or by using a proprietary blueing colourant. These hydrangeas like well-dug soil with added well-rotted garden compost. They also like plenty of moisture; a mulch of humus will help to retain moisture. Do not cut off the old flowerheads once they have faded. Leave them on until mid-spring as winter protection for the young buds.

Propagate by nodal cuttings, taken from late spring to midsummer.

Take care
Keep plants moist.

Hydrangea macrophylla

Lacecap group
- **Light shade**
- **Acid soil**
- **Flowers all summer**

The hydrangeas are among the most useful and accommodating deciduous flowering shrubs. In the Lacecap types the flowerhead consists almost entirely of sterile flowers with a flat disc-like corymb. In the centre there is an area of tiny fertile flowers, and this has a marginal ring of ray flowers which are sterile. 'Blue Wave' is a particularly hardy variety, forming a bush up to 2m (6.5ft) tall and as wide. The large ray flowers have attractive waved edges and vary from pink to blue.

To obtain a really good colour, give 'Blue Wave' very acid conditions and gradual feeding with aluminium. No pruning should be carried out before mid-spring.

Propagate by nodal cuttings, taken from late spring to midsummer.

Take care
Do not prune immediately after flowering; wait until mid-spring. 80▶

Hydrangea paniculata 'Grandiflora'

- Sun or very light shade
- Rich loamy soil
- Summer and autumn flowers

Hydrangea paniculata is a deciduous shrub, or sometimes almost a small tree up to 4.5m (15ft) tall. The cultivar 'Grandiflora', as its name suggests, has even more dramatic-looking flowers than the species *H. paniculata*. Its closely packed cone-like blossoms are at first white, later turning a purplish pink, and finally becoming brown.

To make a first-class bush and superb flowers, this hydrangea needs to be planted in rich loamy soil. Strict pruning gives the best blooms; in spring prune back shoots before new growth starts, and once there are several young shoots, remove the weakest. Finally reduce the bush to about six to ten shoots when they reach 30-71cm (12-28in) high. Mulch with well-rotted farmyard manure after growth has started. Do not overprune by too much thinning, or you will shorten the life of this elegant hydrangea.

Propagate by half-ripe cuttings during mid- to late summer.

Take care
Plant in rich loamy soil.

Hypericum calycinum
(Rose of Sharon; St John's wort; Aaron's beard)

- Full sun or shade
- Well-drained loamy soil
- Flowers in late summer

An almost evergreen low-growing shrub that has creeping rhizomatous growths with an erect habit, which produce unbranched stems 30-45cm (12-18in) high. This superb ground coverer will grow in sun or shade, even in dry situations, provided it has well-drained loamy soils; it does not object to lime in the soil. The large solitary bright yellow flowers, 8cm (3.2in) wide, have a boss of yellow stamens in the centre of each flower.

H. calycinum is the answer where the gardener has a dry bank or an awkward piece of ground where nothing else will grow. Each year in early spring, cut plants back to within 2.5cm (1in) or so of ground level. Where this hypericum clothes large areas, the plants can be cut back with a pair of sharp shears. From time to time it is wise to check this spreader from choking weaker plants growing nearby.

Propagate by divisions in spring.

Take care
Keep plants neat and tidy with an annual clipping.

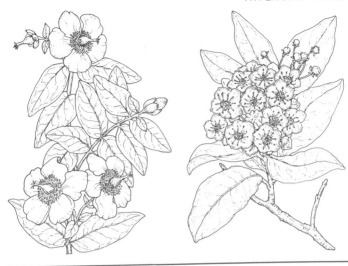

Hypericum 'Hidcote'

- Full sun
- Well-drained loamy soil; tolerates alkaline soils
- Flowers midsummer to autumn

This almost evergreen hypericum may be a hybrid of garden origin between *H. forrestii* and *H. calycinum*. From midsummer to autumn its saucer-shaped golden-yellow flowers, up to 8cm (3.2in) across and each with a central boss of orange anthers, are a lovely sight. The lance-shaped leaves, 4cm (1.6in) long, are pointed at the apex, dark green above and pale grey-green beneath, barely stalked and oppositely arranged around reddish stems. Bushes will reach a height of 1.5m (5ft) and 1.5-2.1m (5-7ft) wide.

Although this bush is quite hardy in cold areas, the young wood may become damaged by frost. If it does not flower very well, prune it hard each spring; cut back last year's growth to its base and remove any weak shoots.

Propagate by softwood cuttings in summer, or by hardwood cuttings in autumn inserted out of doors.

Take care
Prune annually for vigorous plants and abundant flowers. 78-9◊

Kalmia latifolia

(Calico bush; Mountain laurel)
- Full sun or light shade
- Moist fertile peaty soil; not chalk or lime
- Early summer flowering

Surely one of the most beautiful evergreen shrubs, with an affinity to a rhododendron, and a lover of acid peaty soil. A single specimen can reach a height of 3m (10ft) with a similar width. Its large oval leathery leaves are a rich glossy green. A well-grown bush forms dense thickets. The pink ten-ribbed flowers each one like the inside of a parasol, are borne in superbly delicate clusters in early summer.

To flourish, this shrub needs moist well-drained peaty soil, above all lime-free – in full sun or light shade. When it fails, the fault is usually unsuitable growing conditions. No regular pruning is needed. Should a bush grow out of hand it will have to be cut hard back in spring, but it then takes time to regenerate new growth.

Propagate by seed sown in spring under glass, but this is not an easy plant to propagate. Half-ripe cuttings taken in late summer can sometimes be successful.

Take care
Give sufficient moisture. 80◊

89

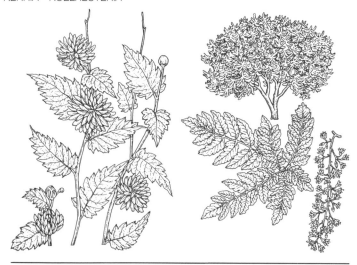

Kerria japonica 'Pleniflora'

(Jew's mallow)
- **Full sun**
- **Any good garden soil, including chalk**
- **Spring flowering**

A useful deciduous hardy shrub, which has apple-green bamboo-like branches and shoots that bear bright orange-yellow double pompom flowers, 4cm (1.6in) across or sometimes more. It will reach a height of 2.5-3m (8-10ft). It spreads very freely by underground stoloniferous roots, which in turn send up new shoots. This vigorous shrub not only has attractive flowers and apple-green branches, but in autumn its leaves turn an attractive light yellow.

   Prune after flowering by cutting flowering wood, and reduce unwanted shoots. Propagate by hardwood cuttings in autumn, or by division of sucker growths in spring.

Take care
Remove all unwanted sucker shoots that appear, before they encroach on other shrubs or perennials. 98♦

Koelreuteria paniculata

(China tree; Golden rain tree; Pride of India; Varnish tree)
- **Full sun**
- **Any good loamy soil**
- **Late summer flowers; autumn foliage**

This handsome slow-growing deciduous ornamental tree can reach 3-4.5m (10-15ft) high, or even up to 9m (30ft). It is a tree that should be grown much more than it is. Its alternate pinnate leaves have nine to 15 leaflets, or sometimes they are bipinnate. The total length of each leaf can be as much as 45cm (18in). The yellow flowers are borne in large terminal pyramidal panicles up to 30cm (12in) long, and produced in late summer. These are followed by bladder-like fruits. In autumn the foliage turns a bright yellow.

   Standard trees can be purchased from reputable nurserymen, with a stem 1.2-1.5m (4-5ft) tall before the head of branches commences. This tree must be grown in full sunshine. No pruning is required, apart from keeping the main stem clean.

   Propagate by seeds sown in spring, or by root cuttings taken in winter and grown under glass.

Take care
Give this tree full sun. 97♦

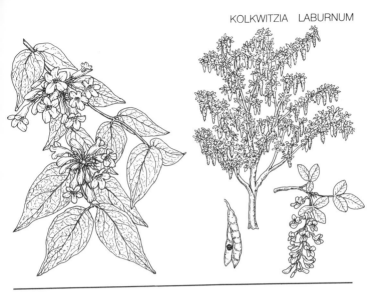

Kolkwitzia amabilis 'Pink Cloud'

(Beauty bush)
- **Sunny position**
- **Any good soil, including chalk**
- **Flowers in spring and early summer**

This handsome deciduous hardy shrub, 2-2.5m (6.5-8ft) high, forms a dense twiggy bush, most suitable for a medium-sized garden. The opposite leaves are roughly oval, and rounded at the base, dull green above and paler beneath. In spring and early summer the arching branches are covered with dense clusters of bell-shaped flowers; the roundish lobes are pink, the throat a delicate yellow. One of the best clones produced for garden use is 'Pink Cloud', with the same colouring as the species.

The only pruning needed is to remove old or weak wood as soon as the bushes have finished flowering, but always bear in mind that kolkwitzias should be allowed to grow naturally.

Propagate by taking half-ripe cuttings in summer; insert them in a propagating frame with some bottom heat.

Take care
Do not over-prune. 98♦

Laburnum anagyroides

(Common laburnum)
- **Sunny location**
- **Any garden soil**
- **Flowers in late spring and early summer**

Laburnum is one of the most popular small deciduous flowering trees for a late spring and early summer display of colour. It will reach a height of 5.5-7.6m (18-25ft). The trifoliate leaves have a long stalk and oval leaflets, dull green above and downy beneath. The golden-yellow flowers are borne on downy pendulous racemes, 15-25cm (6-10in) long.

As laburnums bloom so freely they also set seed freely, and this can be a strain on the tree. Therefore as soon as flowering has finished remove the seedpods. Laburnums are not especially long-lived trees. Where there are young children it is a wise precaution to remove the seedpods, because they are poisonous. This is a tree that needs secure staking, especially when young or newly planted. If large branches have to be removed, do this in summer; if it is done in spring, bleeding can occur.

Propagate by seeds in spring.

Take care
Stake trees securely. 99♦

91

Laburnum × watereri

- **Sunny location**
- **Any garden soil**
- **Early summer flowering**

This hardy deciduous flowering tree is a hybrid between *L. alpinum* and *L. anagyroides*, and it makes a small compact tree with glossy green trifoliate leaves. It has slender 30cm (12in) racemes of yellow fragrant flowers in early summer. The seeds of laburnum species are poisonous, but *L. × watereri* has the advantage that seed does not set so freely on this hybrid as it does on the common laburnum. Another equally beautiful cross with the same parent as *L. × watereri* is the cultivar 'Vossii', which has even longer racemes of golden-yellow flowers, up to 71cm (28in) long. Trees will reach a height of 9-10.7m (30-35ft).

Like all laburnums, in the early stages of their life they must be given secure staking. Prune as for *L. anagyroides*.

Propagate by grafting onto *L. anagyroides* in spring.

Laurus nobilis

(Bay; Bay laurel; Poet's laurel; Sweet bay)
- **Sunny location**
- **Any well-drained soil**
- **Spring flowering**

This handsome aromatic evergreen tree or large shrub from the Mediterranean has leathery foliage, dark green above, paler beneath. The leaves are finely crinkled, and the bark is dark grey-black. In spring it bears pale yellow pleasantly scented flowers in the axils of the alternate leaves. At first, trees may be slow-growing, but eventually they grow freely and can reach a height of 6-12.2m (20-40ft).

They are excellent in seaside areas and make good shelter. In very hard winters foliage may be damaged by frost, but this will soon recover. The tree stands up to clipping, and if necessary this can be carried out several times during the summer. A sharp pair of secateurs should be used.

Propagate by hardwood cuttings taken in late summer or early autumn and inserted in a cold frame.

Take care
Stake trees securely. 100♦

Take care
Keep trees neatly trimmed.

Lavandula 'Hidcote'

(Lavender)
- **Full sun**
- **Light, not too rich soil, including chalky soils**
- **Early summer flowering**

The evergreen low-growing fragrant-foliaged early-flowering lavenders, such as 'Hidcote' and 'Munstead', are very useful for a small garden, either as a clump of three or four plants, or as a low edging or hedge by a flower border, especially around rosebeds. 'Hidcote' will reach a height of 25-38cm (10-15in), forming a compact small bush. It has narrow grey-green foliage, and stems which in early summer produce close spikes of violet-coloured flowers.

Lavenders thrive best on a light, not-too-rich soil and grow well in chalk or lime soils. The best time to prune lavender is in the spring, but do not prune immediately after flowering, because the old growth protects the young growth, which will produce the next year's crop of flowers.

Propagate by taking heel or nodal cuttings of ripened wood; insert them in sandy soil in a cold frame in late summer.

Take care
Do not prune after flowering, but wait until the following spring. 100-101♦

Leycesteria formosa

(Flowering nutmeg; Grandma's curls; Himalayan honeysuckle)
- **Full sun or partial shade**
- **Any rich fertile soil**
- **Flowers from early summer to early autumn**

This hardy deciduous shrub has pinkish white pendent flowers surrounded by claret-coloured bracts, which are produced from early summer to early autumn. They are followed by clusters of reddish purple berries like small gooseberries, in autumn. The hollow green bamboo-like stems are enhanced by opposite leaves, which are green above and paler beneath, attached to wine-red stalks. It is a native of the shady forests of the Himalayas and Tibet.

Provided it has a rich soil, this shrub will reach a height of 2m (6.5ft) at least, and 1.2m (4ft) in width. The only pruning needed is to thin out the older and weaker shoots down to ground level in spring. Also cut back any shoots that have been frosted, to healthy growth.

Propagate by seeds sown in spring, or by hardwood cuttings in autumn.

Take care
Trim bushes if frost has taken its toll.

Ligustrum lucidum

(Chinese privet; Chinese wax-flower; Shining-leaved privet)

- **Sunny position**
- **Any good fertile soil**
- **Flowers late summer and early autumn**

This is an evergreen small tree or large shrub; it makes a tree that can reach 6-9m (20-30ft) tall, though more frequently it is only 3-5.5m (10-18ft) high; the larger dimensions would only be found in old and well-established trees. As a rule privet flowers are not welcome, but those of *L. lucidum* are extremely fragrant when they appear in large erect terminal panicles during late summer and early autumn. The foliage is also large, and the narrow oval leaves are a dark lustrous green.

No pruning is needed. Propagate by layering the previous season's growth in spring; obviously such an operation would have to be performed for a bush.

Take care

Be sure to buy the correct tree or shrub; *L. lucidum* is sometimes confused with *L. japonicum*, which is a much smaller evergreen privet.

Ligustrum ovalifolium 'Aureum'

(Golden privet)

- **Sunny position**
- **Any good fertile soil**
- **Coloured foliage throughout the year**

This evergreen shrub (occasionally almost semi-evergreen) is a golden-leaved cultivar of the common privet. It makes an attractive bush, and its colourful golden-yellow foliage brightens gardens in the dull winter months. The opposite leaves on brown stems are 4-4.5cm (1.6-1.8in) long. Each leaf has a green centre with golden-yellow margins of varying width; some leaves are almost entirely yellow. This shrub may grow 3-3.6m (10-12ft) tall. The foliage is useful for floral arrangements.

Privet will tolerate any good fertile soil, but to give of its best it must have full sun. It can be pruned at any time during the summer, but if hard pruning is necessary, do this in late spring, when new shoots will soon be thrown up from the base.

Propagate by hardwood cuttings in autumn, inserted out of doors.

Take care

Remove any shoots that revert to green to maintain gold colour.

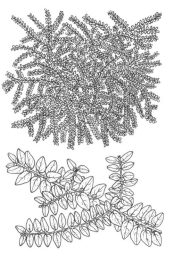

Lonicera nitida 'Baggesen's Gold'

- Full sun
- Any good garden soil
- Summer and autumn foliage

Lonicera × purpusii

- Full sun
- Any good garden soil
- Winter flowering

This golden-leaved hardy evergreen shrub will reach a height of 1.2-1.5m (4-5ft) and just over 1m (39in) wide. The small opposite leaves are almost oval, 1.2cm (0.5in) long, heart-shaped at the base and blunt at the apex. Throughout the summer they are golden-yellow in colour, but during the autumn and winter they turn to a yellowish green.

If three to five plants are grown as a clump they will make a bright addition to the garden in summer and autumn; they are not quite as bright as golden privet in winter, but still worth growing. To keep bushes shapely, trim them when necessary during the summer. Should they become overgrown and ill-shapen, then hard pruning in spring will soon improve their appearance.

Propagate by hardwood cuttings in mid-autumn, inserted out of doors.

Take care
Keep bushes tidy by trimming them when necessary.

This attractive deciduous hardy flowering shrub is a hybrid between *L. fragantissima* and *L. standishii*. The creamy-white fragrant flowers, in clusters of two to four, are carried in the axils of the opposite foliage. The leaves are oval in shape, 5-9cm (2-3.5in) long and 3-4.5cm (1.2-1.8in) wide, somewhat rounded at the base and edged with bristly hairs. The joy about this shrub is that it gives flowers and fragrance during late winter. It is also taller than either of its parents and will reach a height of up to 3m (10ft) and larger in width.

The only pruning needed is to thin and shorten any extra-long branches after flowering has finished.

Propagate by taking cuttings of mature wood of the current season's growth, with or without a heel, and about 20-30cm (8-12in) long; insert out of doors in an open border.

Take care
Keep this vigorous shrub within bounds. 101♦

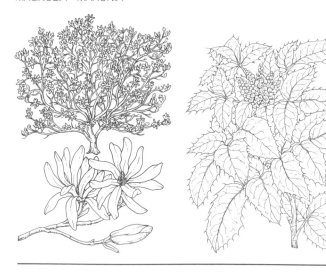

Magnolia stellata
(Star magnolia)
- **Sunny position**
- **Good loam or peaty soil**
- **Spring flowering**

This is the ideal deciduous shrub for a small garden where a magnolia is desired. It makes a compact rounded shrub, 2.5-3.6m (8-12ft) tall and as much or sometimes more in width. The long narrow oblong leaves are 6.5-10cm (2.5-4in) in length. In spring the bush produces fragrant, pure white strap-like flowers, each flower having 12 to 18 petals.

This plant needs a sunny position and a good loamy soil, with added leaf-mould, peat and sand if the ground is at all wet or inclined to drain badly. Initial preparation prior to planting is essential. Newly planted bushes will take up to two years to establish. This species is easily blackened by frost, so try to plant it in a sheltered position. No pruning is necessary.

Propagate this superb shrub by layering in early spring.

Take care
Choose a sheltered situation to avoid frost damage. 102♦

Mahonia aquifolium
(Oregon grape)
- **Sun or shade**
- **Any soil, including lime**
- **Spring flowering**

This hardy evergreen shrub does well in full sun or shade, provided the shade is not too dense. It has no affinity with a vine, but gets its common name because of its clusters of deep blue-black berries, with a violet-purple bloom. Dense racemes of golden-yellow flowers are borne in terminal clusters in spring. It has pinnate leaves 15-30cm (6-12in) long, with five to nine leaflets and almost stalkless. The glossy dark green foliage, sometimes tinged with bronze, turns purplish crimson in autumn and winter. This superb ground cover plant spreads by underground suckers, reaching a height of 60-90cm (24-36in) or taller, and 1-1.5m (39in-5ft) in width.

Little attention is needed apart from going over clumps in spring, after flowering, and cutting back strong growths close to ground level.

Propagate by seed or by division of suckers, in spring.

Take care
Keep plants within bounds by trimming them in spring.

Above: **Koelreuteria paniculata**
These handsome pinnate leaves can be 45cm (18in) long. In late summer, this medium-sized tree bears impressive clusters of bright yellow flowers. Grow it in full sun. 90♦

Above: **Kerria japonica 'Pleniflora'**
Charming double yellow spring blooms on bright green stems make this a popular hardy shrub. 90♦

Below: **Kolkwitzia amabilis 'Pink Cloud'**
The variety name aptly describes this early summer floral display. 91♦

Above: **Laburnum anagyroides**
Trained over a garden pergola, these pendulous racemes of late spring flowers form a striking floral canopy. A handsome tree but beware – all parts of it are poisonous. 91▶

Left: **Laburnum × watereri**
In an open sunny location, this compact garden tree puts on a marvellous show of pendulous yellow flowers in early summer. As a bonus, the flowers are fragrant and rarely set seed. Stake young trees. 92♦

Right: **Lonicera × purpusii**
Creamy white fragrant flowers are carried on almost bare branches in late winter. This shrub grows vigorously and must be kept in check by pruning after flowering is over. Flourishes in full sun. 95♦

Below: **Lavandula 'Hidcote'**
The heady fragrance of the lavender's flowers and foliage is reason enough to recommend it for garden use. Excellent as an edging plant on light soils in open sunny locations. 93♦

Above: **Magnolia stellata**
*This compact slow-growing
deciduous shrub bears a splendid*

*display of creamy white fragrant
flowers in spring. Grow it in a good
soil with leaf-mould and peat.* 96♦

Above: **Mahonia japonica**
This evergreen shrub will grow quite happily in light shade. Its pale yellow fragrant flowers appear in winter. 113♦

Below: **Malus floribunda**
Securely staked in fertile soil, this semi-weeping tree abounds with spring bloom and autumn fruit. 113♦

Right: **Osmanthus delavayi**
*These white flowers, superbly
fragrant and shown off well by the
dark green foliage, appear in early
spring. The shrub grows in almost any
soil and situation, reaching 3m (10ft)
in height and width. Give protection
from spring frost.* 116♦

Below right: **Morus alba 'Pendula'**
*This weeping form of the white
mulberry makes a striking garden
feature. For a non-weeping mulberry
choose Morus nigra, which has
catkin-like spring flowers followed by
dark purple autumn fruits. In winter,
the attractive dark orange bark
provides interest until the foliage and
flowers appear.* 114♦

Below: **Osmanthus × burkwoodii**
*Similar to Osmanthus delavayi, this
hybrid has dark glossy leaves and is
hardier. It grows slowly into a dense
bush up to 3.6m (12ft) in height and
width. It thrives in any soil, including
chalk, and can stand light shade.* 116♦

Above: **Paeonia suffruticosa
'Rock's Variety'**
*These stunning 15cm (6in) blooms
are produced during the spring. 117♦*

Below: **Pernettya mucronata**
*Abundant berries smother this hardy
evergreen shrub during the winter.
Colour depends on variety. 117♦*

Above:
Philadelphus coronarius 'Aureus'
The combination of golden-yellow *foliage and sweetly scented creamy* *white summer flowers makes this a* *highly desirable garden shrub.* 118♦

Left: Philadelphus 'Manteau d'Hermine'
This is one of several excellent hybrids. It bears double creamy white flowers during the summer that scent the whole garden. 118♦

Right: Prunus laurocerasus 'Otto Luyken'
Extremely useful as ground cover, this low-growing evergreen shrub bears abundant terminal flower clusters in spring. It will flourish in the shade of trees. 121♦

Below: Potentilla 'Elizabeth'
This shrubby potentilla puts on a magnificent show of colour from late spring until early autumn. A hardy dependable plant for sun or partial shade and in any soil. Cut out old stems for vigorous growth. 121♦

Above: **Prunus lusitanica**
*Here grown as a standard tree, the
Portugal laurel can also form a dense
bush. It will thrive on any type of soil,
including chalk, and looks best when
grown as a specimen plant.* 122▸

Above: **Prunus sargentii**
These single pink flowers appear in early spring as the young coppery leaves begin to develop. 122♦

Below: **Prunus 'Cheal's Weeping'**
A graceful Japanese cherry adorned with double pink flowers in spring. Excellent for small gardens. 123♦

Above: **Prunus subhirtella 'Pendula'**
Spring sunshine playing on these delicate pale pink flowers creates a superb spectacle in a small garden. Give this weeping tree an open site. 124◀

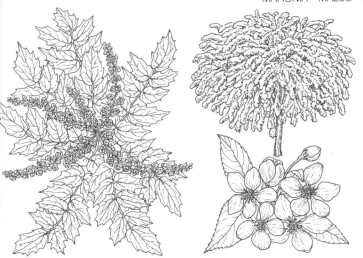

Mahonia japonica
- **Sun or dappled shade**
- **Good loam or peaty soil**
- **Winter flowering**

Malus floribunda
(Japanese crab)
- **Fun sun**
- **Any fertile soil**
- **Spring flowering**

This evergreen shrub is probably one of the most popular because it flowers in winter. The lemon-yellow fragrant flowers, 20-25cm (8-10in) long, are borne on pendulous racemes in clusters of ten or more at the tips of the previous year's growth. The leaves, dark green above and yellowish beneath, are 30-45cm (12-18in) long with 13 to 19 leaflets, each spine-tipped at the apex. When first planted, bushes seem slow to start; but once established they soon put on growth and eventually reach a height of 1.5-2.1m (5-7ft). This is a stiff-growing shrub and sparsely branched, but when well grown it is an asset to any shrub border.

No regular pruning is needed, but a few sprays cut and brought indoors encourage plenty of new growth.

Propagate by taking half-ripe cuttings of the current year's growth during summer, making them about 15cm (6in) long.

A deciduous flowering tree with a semi-weeping habit that forms a small rounded spreading tree with arching branches. In spring the bare branches produce small rosy-red buds, which later become pale pink flowers, up to 3-3.5cm (1.2-1.4in) across and carried in clusters of four to seven, on stalks 3-4cm (1.2-1.6in) long. In autumn there are small round red and yellow berry-like fruits. It has oval leaves on the weaker shoots, but on stronger shoots there are three- to five-lobed leaves, dullish green above and paler beneath.

Initial preparation of the soil is very important, and newly planted trees should be securely staked. Once the tree is well-established, little or no pruning is needed.

Propagate by budding in summer, or by grafting onto the common Crab apple, *Malus pumila* in spring.

Take care
Give this mahonia ample room to spread naturally. 103♦

Take care
Remove all suckers that arise below the union, ie where the budding or grafting has been performed. 103♦

Malus tschonoskii

(Pillar apple)

- **Full sun**
- **Any fertile soil**
- **Spring flowers, autumn foliage**

An exceptionally colourful deciduous tree of erect pyramidal formation with broadly oval or rounded leaves, 5-13cm (2-5in) long and 4-8cm (1.6-3.2in) wide, and grey-felted beneath. In spring, large white flowers, at first rose-tinted, and 2.5-3.5cm (1-1.4in) across, are produced in clusters of four to six; these are followed in autumn by globose, 2.5cm (1in) wide, fruits of brownish yellow and flushed a purplish crimson. The final glory of the Pillar apple is the turning of its foliage in autumn through bronze to brilliant blood-red, streaked with vivid crimson-scarlet. Although trees will reach a height of 9-12.2m (30-40ft), their erect conical shape makes them very suitable for the small or medium-sized garden.

Little, if any, pruning is needed. Propagate by budding in summer, or by grafting in spring, onto the common Crab apple, *Malus pumila*.

Take care

Remove all suckers that arise below the union, ie where the budding or grafting has been performed.

Morus nigra

(Common mulberry; Black mulberry)

- **Full sun**
- **Well-drained loamy soil**
- **Spring or early summer flowering; fruit in late summer**

The common mulberry is a gnarled deciduous tree, with dark orange bark. The coarsely toothed lobed oval leaves are heart-shaped at the base, glossy rough green above and paler and downy below. The small self-fertile greenish yellow catkin-like flowers are produced in spring or early summer, and followed by globose raspberry-like fruits in late summer, first green, then dark red to purplish black. Mulberry trees can grow to 6-9m (20-30ft) in height and often as wide. For a weeping mulberry choose *M. alba* 'Pendula'.

The trees grow very slowly and thrive in a warm, well-drained soil. The branches are brittle, and prone to bleeding when cut; any thinning needed should be done in early winter.

Propagate by hardwood cuttings of the current year's growth, 25-30cm (10-12in) long with a heel, inserted out of doors in winter.

Take care

Plant in a carefully chosen site, as the fruit can be messy when it drops. 105♦

Myrtus communis
(Common myrtle)
- **Sunny sheltered location**
- **Any soil, including chalk**
- **Summer flowering**

An evergreen shrub hardy only in sheltered situations and ideal for seaside locations. Its opposite small leaves are oval to lance-shaped, dark glossy green above and paler beneath. The foliage is fragrant when crushed. This shrub has a profusion of solitary, creamy white fragrant flowers, 2cm (0.8in) across. It was a favourite of the ancients, who considered it sacred to the goddess of love, and even to this day sprigs of myrtle are included in many wedding bouquets. The flowers are followed by purple-black berries. Bushes will reach a height of 2-2.7m (6.5-9ft).

No pruning is needed, unless it is necessary to restrict its growth, in which case the taller branches can be cut back in spring. If the bush is badly damaged by frost, it will in most cases break freely from the old wood at the base.

Propagate by taking half-ripe cuttings with a heel during the summer.

Take care
Protect myrtle against frost damage by growing it in a sheltered position.

Olearia × haastii
(Daisy bush)
- **Sunny position**
- **Any soil, including chalk**
- **Summer flowering**

This bushy evergreen shrub is the hardiest of the olearias; it has a rounded habit, and reaches 1.2-2.7m (4-9ft) tall and 2-2.5m (6.5-8ft) wide. The alternate oval leaves are crowded on its branches; each leaf is 1.2-2.5cm (0.5-1in) long and nearly half as wide, dark shining green above and white felted beneath. The daisy-like white flowers are carried above the foliage, forming flattish clusters 5-7.5cm (2-3in) across. Each flower is made up of white ray florets and yellow disc florets.

For newly planted bushes, only light pruning is necessary in the first few years. If bushes become tall and stems bare, then during spring cut such stems well back into the old wood; plants will soon regenerate from the base.

Propagate by taking half-ripe cuttings in late summer or early autumn

Take care
Keep bushes tidy by cutting them back if they become leggy.

Osmanthus × burkwoodii

(syn. Osmarea × burkwoodii)
- Sun or light shade
- Any good loamy or chalk soil
- Spring flowering

Osmanthus delavayi

- Sun or light shade
- Any good loamy or chalk soil
- Spring flowering

This hardy evergreen shrub was originally known as a bigeneric hybrid between *Osmanthus delavayi* and *Phillyrea decora*; but since the second parent is now called *Osmanthus decorus*, botanists have decreed that the shrub is a hybrid between *O. delavayi* and *O. decorus*. Whichever name it is sold under, buy it, for it is a real beauty. It has glossy oval dark olive-green toothed leaves, 2.5-5cm (1-2in) long. The terminal and axillary clusters of six or seven fragrant white flowers are produced in spring; they are not so sweetly scented as *O. delavayi*, but hardier. It is rather slow in growth, but eventually makes a dense bushy shrub, 2.7-3.6m (9-12ft) in height and equally wide. It is a very desirable and useful evergreen.

Any pruning needed should be done once flowering has finished. Propagate by half-ripe cuttings, in late spring or early summer.

This evergreen shrub has sweetly scented flowers. It is hardy except in the very coldest and frostiest areas, where it should be grown against a wall or fence. It has small dark green leathery leaves, with tiny dark spots beneath; the leaves are oval in shape and tapered at each end. In spring it has pure white fragrant jasmine-like flowers, which are produced in terminal and axillary clusters. In favoured localities it will reach a height of 3m (10ft), and sometimes more in overall width.

Plant this shrub where it will have protection from the ovrhanging branches of a nearby tree, or in a position where the sun will not reach the bush before the frost is off, so that damage to the flowers will be less. Any pruning needed should be done after flowering.

Propagate by half-ripe cuttings in late summer.

Take care
Give plenty of room to expand. 104♦

Take care
Plant this shrub where it has some protection. 104-5♦

Paeonia suffruticosa
(Moutan paeony; Tree paeony)
- **Some shade is preferable**
- **Any good garden soil**
- **Spring flowering**

Pernettya mucronata
- **Full sun or partial shade**
- **Moist loamy lime-free soil**
- **Spring and summer flowers; autumn and winter berries**

This hardy deciduous flowering shrub is a slow grower, eventually reaching a height of 1.2-1.5m (4-5ft), sometimes 2m (6.5ft) and equally wide. It has gnarled twisted branches with elegant foliage; the doubly pinnate or double ternate leaves are 23-45cm (9-18in) long, dark to mid-green above and bluish grey beneath. The 15cm (6in) wide flowers are white with a maroon-purple blotch at the base of each petal. *P.s.* 'Rock's Variety' is similar in colour.

Tree paeonies need a protected position so that the early morning sun does not harm the blooms before any frost on them has thawed. Paeonies need rich well-cultivated soil with liberal mulchings of leaf-mould or well-rotted farmyard manure. The only pruning necessary is to remove any dead wood after flowering. Propagate by grafting onto rootstocks of *P. officinalis* in spring.

Take care
Shade paeonies to prevent frost damage. 106♦

Surely one of the most decorative hardy evergreen shrubs. It has nodding cylindrical white flowers produced singly in the leaf axils in spring and summer, followed by 1cm (0.4in) berries in autumn and winter in varying colours of pure white to lilac-pink, purple, crimson and red. The branches are densely covered with alternate shining dark green toothed leaves ending in a sharp point.

It tolerates sun but is equally happy in partial shade. Its chief needs are a moist gritty sand-peat soil.

One male should be planted for up to four or five female bushes in order to have berries, as the sexes are on different plants. There are, however, hermaphrodite forms such as 'Bell's Seedling' and Davis's Hybrids. No regular pruning is needed.

Propagate by seeds, by suckers, or by cuttings in late summer or early autumn.

Take care
Grow in lime-free soil. 106♦

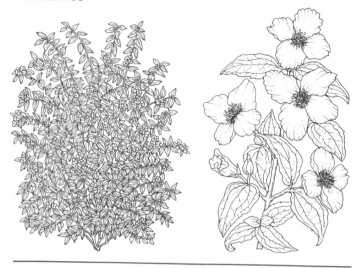

Philadelphus coronarius 'Aureus'

(Golden-leaved mock orange; Syringa)
- **Full sun**
- **Any good garden soil**
- **Summer flowering**

This hardy deciduous shrub is one of the sweetest scented shrubs. 'Aureus' is the golden-leaved cultivar; in spring the foliage is a bright golden-yellow, but it becomes duller after midsummer. The oval lance-shaped leaves are 4-8cm (1.6-3.2in) long, and slightly toothed. The creamy white sweetly scented flowers in summer makes this golden beauty an ideal fragrant shrub.

It rarely grows to more than 2.7m (9ft), so it is ideal for the small or medium-sized garden. Do not provide too rich a soil, and it will tolerate chalk soils; it is a good shrub for growing in coastal areas. As the flowers are produced on the previous year's shoots, pruning should be carried out as soon as the flowers are over; cut back old flowering wood to strong new growths.

Propagate by hardwood cuttings in autumn, and insert out of doors.

Take care
Remove old worn-out shoots from time to time 107♦

Philadelphus modern hybrids

(Mock orange; Syringa)
- **Full sun**
- **Any good garden soil**
- **Summer flowering**

Over the years many beautiful hybrid varieties of philadelphus have been raised and introduced. The following are worthy of space in a small or medium-sized garden. 'Belle Etoile' has fragrant white flowers with a reddish blotch in the centre of each flower; its height is 1.5-2m (5-6.5ft). 'Sybille; has large saucer-shaped fragrant flowers up to 5cm (2in) wide, borne singly or in twos or threes; the blooms are purplish white at the base of each petal, with sea-green foliage, and the shrub is 1.2-2m (4-6.5ft) tall. A third beauty is the double or semi-double white cup-shaped fragrant 'Virginal', which reaches 2-2.5m (6.5-8ft) tall. The compact 'Manteau d'Hermine', with creamy white fragrant flowers borne usually in threes, is about 1m (39in) tall.

The general care and cultivation, pruning and propagation of all these varieties are exactly the same as for *P. coronarius* 'Aureus'.

Take care
Remove old stems as necessary. 108♦

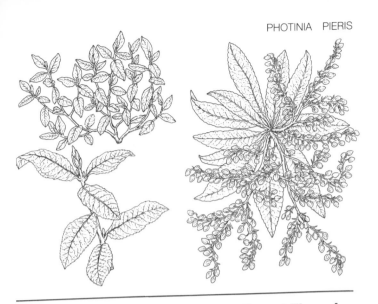

Photinia × fraseri 'Red Robin'
- **Full sun**
- **Warm fertile soil, including chalky soils**
- **Spring and summer foliage**

This ornamental hardy evergreen shrub was at first thought to be a form of *Photinia glabra*, but is now classed as a hybrid between *P. glabra* and *P. serrulata*. The leaves are dark glossy green above and paler beneath, a yellowish green with a stalk 2.5cm (1in) or more long. The leaves are up to 10cm (4in) long and 6.5cm (2.5in) wide. The leaves are shallowly toothed with a blunt point at the apex. In spring the foliage is brilliant red and remains so well into the summer. The shrub reaches 3m (10ft) in height.

Although this plant grows happily on acid soils, its colour is even more brilliant on chalky soils. In spring, if foliage is cut back, fresh red foliage will soon appear.

Propagate by half-ripe heel cuttings in summer, or by hardwood cuttings in autumn.

Take care
Give this shrub full sun.

Pieris 'Forest Flame'
- **Sun with overhead shade**
- **Peaty soil or lime-free loam**
- **Spring flowers and foliage**

An evergreen hardy shrub, reaching at least 2m (6.5ft) in height, with attractive flowers and coloured foliage in spring. The oblong lance-like leaves, with a narrowly tapered base, are up to 13cm (5in) long by 3cm (1.2in) wide. 'Forest Flame' comes into growth earlier than the cultivar 'Wakehurst', but the elegant foliage is less vivid; even so, the young growths are at first brilliant red, later changing through pink to creamy white, and finally to green. The white pitcher-shaped flowers are produced in a cluster of panicles and borne at the end of the previous year's shoots.

'Forest Flame' needs a light lime-free peaty soil, with light overhead shade and a protected position as it is vulnerable to late spring frosts.

Propagate by seed, by half-ripe heel cuttings in summer, or by layering in autumn.

Take care
Give light shade as protection against late spring frosts. 6♦

Piptanthus laburnifolius

(Evergreen laburnum)

- **Sunny sheltered position**
- **Well-drained or chalky soils**
- **Late spring flowering**

This almost evergreen shrub, deciduous in severe winters, is best planted with the protection of a wall or fence. It will reach a height of 2-2.5m (6.5-8ft). The alternate foliage consists of trifoliate lance-like stalkless leaflets, 8-15cm (3.2-6in) long and about 3-5cm (1.2-2in) wide, dark green above and bluish grey beneath. In late spring bright yellow laburnum-like flowers are produced and borne on erect stiff racemes 5-8cm (2-3.2in) long.

Although this is a vigorous shrub, it is not long-lived, but can be easily renewed from seeds, which are freely produced. It dislikes root disturbance, so always use pot-grown plants. In mild areas it will remain evergreen, but in colder areas it is often deciduous. Bushes should be allowed to grow freely; if they are badly frosted, prune hard back in spring, tipping back uninjured healthy branches. Propagate from seed sown in spring, or from half-ripe cuttings in summer.

Take care
Give some protection.

Pittosporum tenuifolium

(Kohuhu)

- **Sunny location**
- **Well-drained soil**
- **Spring flowering**

This is a handsome evergreen tree or outsized bush growing to 9m (30ft), and therefore suitable only for medium-sized gardens. The pale shining green wavy-edged foliage, paler beneath, is attractive at all seasons, and is carried on black twigs. In spring in favoured localities, especially near the sea, chocolate and purple flowers are produced in the leaf axils, and they have a honey-like fragrance, strongest in the evenings.

Bushes can easily be kept in control by drastic pruning in spring; they will regenerate freely from the old wood. The foliage is used extensively by florists, especially during the winter months. In less favourble areas, after frost damage, this species will have to be cut well back. Two attractive cultivars are 'Silver Queen', with pale green leaves margined with white, and 'Warnham Gold', with golden-yellow foliage.

Propagate by half-ripe cuttings in summer, or by seeds in spring.

Take care
Choose a sheltered site.

Potentilla 'Elizabeth'
(Cinquefoil)
- **Sun or partial shade**
- **Any good soil**
- **Flowers from late spring to early autumn**

The shrubby potentillas are hardy and free-flowering; there are many varieties and hybrids. 'Elizabeth' is probably a hybrid between *P. arbuscula* and *P. dahurica* var *veitchii*; and originally it was grown under the species *P. arbuscula*. This deciduous dome-shaped bush is about 1m (39in) high, and as much in width; from late spring to early autumn it is adorned with large rich primrose-yellow strawberry-like flowers up to 4cm (1.6in) in diameter. Today there are many potentillas to choose from; 'Katherine Dykes' has primrose-yellow flowers, and 'Red Ace' has vermilion-flame backed by pale yellow flowers and is only 50cm (20in) high.

To keep potentillas vigorous, occasionally remove old worn-out stems down to ground level. They thrive in any good garden soil, and do well in full sun, but also tolerate partial shade. Propagate by seeds in late winter, or by half-ripe cuttings in late summer.

Take care
Remove worn-out stems. 108-9♦

Prunus laurocerasus 'Otto Luyken'
- **Sun or dappled shade**
- **Good fertile soil; not chalk soils**
- **Spring flowering**

A fine low-growing hardy evergreen 1-1.2m (3.3-4ft) tall with a spread of (eventually) 2.1-2.7m (7-9ft). It has glossy deep green leathery foliage, the leaves almost 2.5cm (1in) wide, and pointed at either end; they are thickly set on ascending branches, which grow at a semi-erect angle from the ground. This free-flowering variety produces vertical terminal racemes of white flowers. It is an outstanding evergreen especially for small or medium-sized gardens, and it is ideal as a ground cover shrub.

Normally pruning will not be necessary, but if it has to be done, choose spring or early summer.

Propagate by hardwood cuttings during the summer inserted out of doors in a border facing away from the sun.

Take care
Give room to spread naturally. 109♦

121

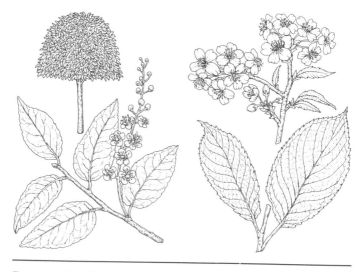

Prunus lusitanica
(Portugal laurel)
- **Sun or dappled shade**
- **Warm well-drained soil**
- **Early summer flowering and foliage**

This handsome evergreen shrub needs to be grown as an isolated specimen where its rich green glossy foliage can be appreciated. In early summer it produces a mass of long slender racemes of dull white flowers, followed later by a profusion of small purple cherries. From time to time specimens are trained so that they have a broad squat head of foliage on a short stem; old specimens eventually have a stout trunk. Bushes or standard trees can be anything from 3-4.5m (10-15ft) tall, with a spread of 4.5m (15ft) or even wider.

When pruning is needed, this should be done in spring or early summer. The cultivar 'Variegata' has leaves margined with white, and in winter the foliage is often flushed with pink. A large specimen can grow 1.5-2m (5-6.5ft) tall, and somewhat wider.

Propagate by hardwood cuttings in autumn, inserted out of doors.

Take care
Cut out any shoots that have silver leaf, and treat wounds with a fungicidal pruning paint. 110♦

Prunus sargentii
(Sargent cherry)
- **Sunny position**
- **Any fertile loamy neutral soil**
- **Spring flowering**

This splendid deciduous ornamental cherry reaches 7.6-10.7m (25-35ft) with a spread of 5.5-7.6m (18-25 ft); these measurements are for mature trees. The oval, sharply toothed slender pointed leaves are 5-10cm (2-4in) long and half as wide. The young foliage is coppery red, changing to orange-scarlet in early autumn. The tree flowers early in spring. Its large deep blush-pink single flowers, 3.5-4cm (1.4-1.6in) across, are borne in clusters of two to six on long stalks. The bark is a pleasing dark chestnut-brown.

Plant *Prunus sargentii* in an open sunny position where its superb floral display can be seen to advantage. Any pruning necessary should be done either just before or just after flowering.

Propagate by budding in summer, or by grafting in spring.

Take care
Remove suckers from the stock. 111♦

Prunus 'Sato Zakura'

(Japanese cherries)
- **Full sun**
- **Any well-drained soil**
- **Spring flowering**

The following two Japanese cherries are especially suitable for small and medium-sized gardens. The erect *Prunus* 'Amanogawa' is a columnar tree which can eventually become 5m (16.4ft) tall. At first the young foliage is yellowish, before turning green; in early to mid-spring this tree is bedecked with fragrant semi-double soft pink flowers, and in autumn it has coloured foliage.

Where an attractive pendulous tree is wanted, grow 'Cheal's Weeping'. This small tree has attractive arching branches covered with deep pink double flowers. The young leaves are bronze-green, changing later to a glossy green; it is also colourful in autumn. Mature specimens can be 4.5m (15ft) or taller. To encourage this cherry to flower freely, pinch out the tips of all lateral shoots when they are 1-1.2m (39in-4ft) long. Propagate both these cherries by budding in the summer, or by grafting in early spring onto appropriate stocks.

Take care
Remove unwanted shoots which appear below the graft union. 111♦

Prunus serrula

(Mahogany-barked cherry)
- **Full sun**
- **Any fertile loamy neutral soil**
- **Colourful bark all year round**

This deciduous species is a semi-erect cherry 6-7m (20-23ft) high; eventually the arching branches form a broad-headed tree. The willow-like foliage is 5-10cm (2-4in) long; the leaves are slenderly pointed and finely toothed. The white flowers are small and insignificant. The rich bark is its great attraction; as the tree matures, the trunk and branches reveal a handsome polished mahogany surface beneath thin papery bark which peels away in horizontal bands, leaving the trunk like a fine piece of Chippendale furniture.

When training a standard tree, remove all side shoots likely to form branches before they become too set. In very hot dry weather, give trees a thorough soaking. Any pruning needed should be done just before or just after flowering. Propagate by budding in summer, or by grafting onto suitable stocks in spring.

Take care
Remove any suckers which arise from the stocks.

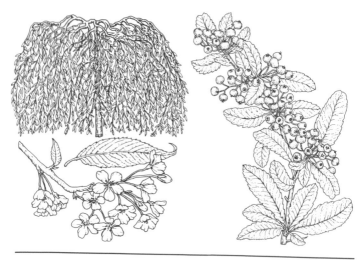

Prunus subhirtella 'Pendula'

(Weeping spring cherry)
- **Full sun**
- **Any fertile loamy neutral soil**
- **Spring flowering**

P. subhirtella 'Pendula' is an excellent pendulous tree for a small garden, as it reaches only 3.6-5.5m (12-18ft) in height with a spread of about 6m (20ft). The tiny pale pink blossoms are freely produced in spring on the base branches of this deciduous weeping tree.

Another form of *P. subhirtella* is the cultivar 'Autumnalis', which grows to 5-6m (16.4-20ft) tall, producing almond-scented semi-double white flowers from late autumn throughout the winter until early spring. It makes a wide-branched small tree with a dense twiggy crown. The autumn apricot tints are very attractive.

No regular pruning is necessary. Propagate by budding in summer, or by grafting onto suitable stocks in spring.

Take care
Remove any suckers which arise from the stocks. 112♦

Pyracantha 'Watereri'

(Firethorn)
- **Prefers sun**
- **All good garden soil, or chalk**
- **Summer flowers; autumn fruits**

Pyracantha 'Watereri' is probably a hybrid between *P. atalantioides* and *P. rogersiana*, the first parent a tall and not so spiny evergreen, the other parent shorter and very spiny; both have an erect habit. 'Watereri' is dense and twiggy, making a vigorous bushy shrub growing to 2.5-3m (8-10ft) in height and at least as wide, sometimes wider. In early summer, bushes are smothered in foamy clusters of white flowers, followed in autumn by masses of bright red berries. This pyracantha makes a handsome free-growing bush, compact and free-fruiting.

Pyracanthas are ideal at the seaside or in industrial areas. The only pruning needed is to keep bushes within bounds; do this in spring.

Propagate by cuttings of the current year's growth with a heel in late summer, or by hardwood cuttings in autumn.

Take care
Wear gloves when pruning. 129♦

Pyrus salicifolia 'Pendula'

(Willow-leaved pear)
- **Full sun**
- **All types of fertile soil; excellent in lime soils**
- **Flowers in late spring**

P. salicifolia 'Pendula' is an excellent tree for a small or medium-sized garden, and looks good even when not in flower. Well-grown standard trees can be anything from 4.5-7.6m (15-25ft) tall, with a spread of 7.6m (25ft) for a mature tree, but it is easy enough to keep them within bounds. Until early summer the foliage is covered with silky white down, later changing to silvery grey, which it keeps until autumn. In spring pure white flowers are produced in small closely packed clusters.

Newly planted specimens will need to be securely staked, especially if the tree has been budded or grafted near the base, but even top-worked trees – those that were budded or grafted to a standard tree stock – will need similar support at first. No pruning is usually necessary.

Propagate by budding in the summer or by grafting in spring, onto suitable stocks.

Take care
Plant only dwarf shrubs beneath this lovely weeping tree.

Rhododendron

Deciduous hybrid azaleas
- **Light shade**
- **Lime-free soil**
- **Late spring and early summer flowering**

These ericaceous shrubs need lime-free soil, peaty, medium or light loams; clay or heavy soils must be lightened. Botanically azaleas are rhododendrons. Ghent 'Nancy Waterer' is large, and a brilliant golden-yellow; Ghent 'Daviesii' is white with a pale yellow eye, and very fragrant; Knap Hill 'Annabella' is bright orange, opening to golden-yellow; and Occidentale 'Irene Koster' is rose pink and fragrant; all four reach 2m (6.5ft). Mollis 'M. Oosthoek' is a deep-orange red; Ghent 'Narcissiflora' is pale yellow and double; both are 1.5m (5ft). Rustica 'Norma' is rose-red with a salmon glow, double, 1.2m (4ft) tall.

On heavy or poor soils work in well-rotted farmyard manure or use leaf-mould or well-moistened peat, and double-dig before planting. No regular pruning is needed.

Propagate by half-ripe cuttings in summer, or by layering in late spring or early summer.

Take care
Remove the seedpods. 131♦

Rhododendron

Evergreen azaleas
- Dappled shade
- Lime-free soil
- Late spring flowering

The evergreen azaleas at one time were all called Japanese azaleas, but over the years they have been so freely hybridized that it is, in our case, sufficient to class them as evergreen azaleas. All are late spring flowering, about 1m (39in) tall and good ground cover plants; the obtusum azaleas have horizontal, dense branches and create wide-spreading shrubs. 'Mikado' is salmon-orange; 'Apple Blossom' has hose in hose flowers, white tinged with pink; 'Hatsugiri' is magenta-purple; 'Hinomayo' is a clear pink; 'Hinodegiri' is bright crimson; 'Shin-seikai', also hose in hose, is white; and 'Amoenum' is very hardy and wide-spreading, rose-purple or brilliant magenta.

They prefer some shade as in full sun their flowers are apt to be scorched. During very dry weather and certainly in times of drought, keep their roots moist. Other particulars as for the deciduous azaleas.

Take care
Remove faded flowerheads. 130◗

Rhododendron

Hardy hybrids
- Full sun or dappled shade
- Well-drained lime-free soil
- Spring and early summer flowering

'Pink Pearl' has large trusses of frilly-edged flesh-pink flowers, paling later; 'Goldsworth Orange' is apricot or orange; and 'Unique' is a pale ochre-yellow flushed with pink; these three are all 2m (6.5ft). 'Britannia', with gloxinia-shaped flowers of cerise scarlet and light green foliage, is 2.5m (8ft). 'Sappho', mauve in bud, later becoming white with dark blotches, is 1.8m (6ft) tall. 'Doncaster' (very hardy) is red with dark spots; and 'Rosy Bell' is apple-blossom pink; both these are 1.5m (5ft) high.

The hardy hybrid rhododendrons are lime-haters, and happiest in moist sandy loam enriched with leaf-mould, moistened peat or well-rotted farmyard manure. Rhododendrons are surface-rooted, so do not plant too deeply. Planting can be done between early autumn and early spring. If they become straggly or too large, prune them back in very late winter or early spring. Propagation is as for deciduous azaleas.

Take care
Remove faded flowerheads. 131◗

 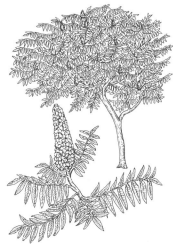

Rhododendron yakushimanum

- **Full sun**
- **Lime-free soil**
- **Spring flowering**

This Japanese dwarf evergreen rhododendron has bell-shaped flowers that are pink in bud, later blush pink, before becoming pure white. The foliage, dark glossy green above, is brown and woolly beneath; the young foliage shoots are silvery white. It develops into a compact bush only 1.2m (4ft) tall and up to 2.1m (7ft) across. The species and several hybrids are in varying shades of pink. 'Golden Torch' is a hybrid with light green foliage; flowers are salmon-pink in bud, changing to chrome yellow. 'Percy Wiseman' is slightly taller yet compact, pink and cream to creamy white. No regular pruning is needed.

Like all rhododendrons, this species must have lime-free soil, but unlike many it also requires full sun.

Propagate by layering during the summer.

Take care
Remove old flower trusses to prevent seedpods forming. 130♦

Rhus typhina
(Stag's-horn sumach)

- **Best in full sun**
- **Any soil, including chalk or lime**
- **Summer flowers, autumn foliage**

This hardy deciduous shrub or small tree has large pinnate foliage, 30-60cm (1-2ft) long, with 13 or more lance-shaped leaflets. The downy green summer leaves change to yellow, rich orange, red or purple in autumn. The branches are covered with reddish brown hairs. There are erect green clusters of male flowers, with smaller female clusters on separate plants. In late autumn the female flowers produce conical crimson hairy fruits.

This shrub produces thickets of suckering shoots, which need to be reduced unless there is ample room for them to spread. Each spring cut surplus shoots down to within an eye or two of the old wood. Bushes can be at least 4.5m (15ft) high, and trees with a short stem reach 4.5-6m (15-20ft).

Propagate by root cuttings in spring, or by removal of suckers in autumn.

Take care
Thin sucker growths annually. 133♦

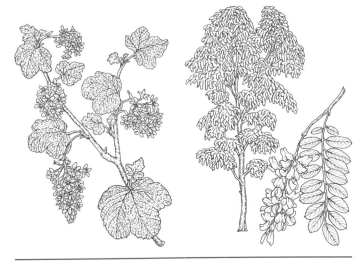

Ribes sanguineum 'Pulborough Scarlet'

(Flowering currant)
- **Sunny position**
- **Any good garden soil**
- **Spring flowering**

Robinia pseudoacacia 'Frisia'

(Common acacia; False acacia)
- **Full sun**
- **Any well-drained soil**
- **Coloured foliage from spring to autumn**

This deciduous spring-flowering shrub has produced a number of cultivars. 'Pulborough Scarlet' has deep red flowers. These make a pleasing contrast to the rich moss-green foliage as it unfolds at the time of flowering. Sprays of 20 to 30 flowers are borne on long wand-like growths. This vigorous shrub reaches a height of 2-2.5m (6.5-8ft) or higher, and as much in width. The palmately three- to five-lobed leaves have a heart-shaped base 5-10cm (2-4in) wide but less in length. This attractive shrub is disliked by some people because of the pungent smell of its flowers and foliage.

Prune by removing an occasional old branch or a few side shoots after flowering has finished.

Propagate by hardwood cuttings, in autumn or winter.

This species will grow into a large tree, which is often seen in industrial areas. The cultivar called 'Frisia' has become very popular, partly because it makes a small to medium-sized tree and is therefore suited to a small or medium-sized garden. It has rich golden-yellow pinnate foliage that creates a superb splash of colour from spring through to autumn. Trees can be anything from 6-8m (20-26ft) high. The thorns on young growths are red, which with the young golden-yellow foliage makes a striking sight.

Any pruning that is necessary should be carried out during mid- or late summer, as there is then less chance of the tree bleeding. Where large wounds are left, treat them with a suitable tree paint.

Propagate by grafting 'Frisia' onto stocks of *R. pseudoacacia* in spring out of doors.

Take care
Give ample room to expand. 133▶

Take care
Treat wounds with a tree paint. 132▶

Above: **Pyracantha 'Watereri'**
Here grown as a wall shrub, this
vigorous evergreen will grow equally
well as a compact bush. These dense
clusters of early summer flowers are
followed by red autumn berries. 124▶

Above:
Rhododendron yakushimanum
A dwarf evergreen with spring flowers
that mature from pink to white. 127♦

Right: **Rhododendron 'Pink Pearl'**
One of the many hardy hybrids
available, this beauty bears large
trusses of frilly pink flowers. 126♦

Below right:
Rhododendron 'Irene Koster'
This is a deciduous hybrid azalea with
lovely fragrant flowers. 125♦

Below:
Rhododendron 'Amoenum'
A hardy, wide-spreading evergreen
azalea for good ground cover. 126♦

131

Above:
Robinia pseudoacacia 'Frisia'
The golden-yellow pinnate foliage *and graceful form of this medium-* *sized tree provide interest from spring* *through to autumn.* 128♦

Above: **Rhus typhina**
The rich autumn tones of this deciduous shrub form a glowing display to enliven any garden. 127♦

Below: **Ribes sanguineum**
Where space permits, this vigorous spring-flowering shrub will grow into a large spreading bush. 128♦

Above: **Rubus Tridel 'Benenden'**
These elegant fragrant flowers, up to 8cm (3.2in) across, appear on arching stems in late spring. 146♦

Below: **Rosa rugosa 'Frau Dagmar Hastrup'**
Perpetual flowering followed by large crimson hips. An ideal hedge. 145♦

Above: **Ruta graveolens**
'Jackman's Blue'
Grown mainly for its attractive blue-green foliage, this evergreen shrub forms a compact bush about 1m (39in) in height and spread. 147▶

Above: **Sarcococca humilis**
Grow this evergreen shrub as ground cover in shady situations. It forms a dense bush only 60cm (2ft) high. The fragrant white flowers appear in late winter and early spring. 148♦

Right: **Senecio 'Sunshine'**
These daisy-like summer flowers stand out well against the grey evergreen foliage. Grow it in full sun on any type of soil. 149♦

Below:
Skimmia japonica 'Rubella'
This male form shows the ruby-red flower buds nestling in the glossy evergreen leaves. These open to white flowers. Female forms produce crops of bright autumn berries. 149♦

Above: **Spiraea thunbergii**
*This spring-flowering deciduous
shrub grows quickly in any good soil
to a height of about 1.5m (5ft). Prune it
after flowering to keep the bush
shapely and vigorous. 151*◗

Above: **Stranvaesia davidiana**
*This large, well-established plant
forms an important feature in this
Italian villa garden. Its white spring
flowerheads are followed in the
autumn by scarlet berries. 153*▶

Above: **Ulex europaeus**
Densely spined and hardy in the most severe conditions, this shrub makes an excellent windbreak or boundary hedge. The bright yellow flowers appear mainly in spring. It will thrive in the poorest of soils. 155♦

Above left: **Styrax japonica**
Hanging bell-shaped blooms adorn this large shrub or small tree in early summer. Grow it in a fertile lime-free soil and provide some protection from spring frost. 154♦

Left: **Viburnum × bodnantense**
These sweetly scented rose-pink flowers are produced during the autumn and winter. They are remarkably frost-resistant. Plant this shrub in an open and sunny position in any fertile soil. 156♦

Above and below:
Viburnum plicatum 'Mariesìi'
The early summer flowers (above) *resemble Lacecap hydrangeas. The branches (below) should be given room to spread horizontally.* 156156♦

Above: **Viburnum tinus**
This evergreen easy-care shrub blooms during the winter and early spring. The white flowers are followed by blue fruits that turn black. A good plant for seaside gardens. 157♦

143

Above: **Weigela 'Bristol Ruby'**
This is one of several hybrids that
provide trouble-free summer colour in
the garden. All enjoy a rich moist soil
and a sunny location. Prune after
flowering each year. 157♦

Rosa rugosa 'Frau Dagmar Hastrup'
- **Sun, but tolerates shade**
- **Most soils; avoid chalk or clay**
- **Perpetual flowering**

R. rugosa 'Frau Dagmar Hastrup' is particularly suitable for the small garden. Like other rugosas it has thick dark green wrinkled foliage. The fairly large rose-pink flowers have a conspicuous centre of creamy yellow stamens; the buds are a rich deep pink. The beautiful blooms are moderately scented and continuously produced. The bush has a compact habit, reaching 1.5m (5ft) tall and 1.2m (4ft) wide. The foliage has splendid autumn colouring, and from summer into autumn there are rich crimson tomato-shaped hips, larger than most. Rugosas are very prickly, and quite impenetrable.

Very little pruning is needed; but if bushes become overcrowded and ungainly, they can be severely cut back in early spring.

Propagate by cuttings 23cm (9in) long, with a heel or cut just below a bud, in autumn or early winter; or remove suckers in autumn.

Take care
Do not over-prune except when rejuvenation is needed. 134◗

Rosmarinus officinalis 'Sissinghurst Blue'
(Rosemary)
- **Rull sun**
- **A light well-drained soil**
- **Late spring flowering**

This lovely evergreen shrub has leaves that are a glossy mid-green above, silvery white beneath, and pungently fragrant. From the opposite tufts of narrow 2cm (0.8in) long leaves, flower buds are formed which produce pretty light blue flowers in late spring. 'Sissinghurst Blue' growing at the foot of the rose 'Helen Knight', which has clear yellow flowers, makes an attractive display. Plants are usually about 1.2m (4ft) high and as wide, but may become taller and wider eventually. The fresh or dried leaves are used as a flavouring with meat, particularly lamb. Pruning is necessary only when bushes become overgrown; in that case cut them back into old wood during the spring.

Propagate by half-ripe cuttings in summer.

Take care
Plant in a sunny sheltered position.

Rubus Tridel 'Benenden'

- **Sun or partial shade**
- **Ordinary well-drained loamy or chalk soil**
- **Late spring flowering**

This deciduous hardy flowering shrub is a hybrid between *Rubus trilobus* and *R. deliciosus* giving it a group name of Tridel, whereas the clone name is 'Benenden'. It has dark green leaves with three to five lobes. This vigorous shrub of the bramble family has spineless stems with peeling bark. The tall arching branches reach a height of 2.5-3m (8-10ft). In late spring the shrub produces many single pure white scented flowers, 6-8cm (2.3-3.2in) across, each flower with a central boss of golden-yellow stamens.

Pruning consists of cutting out the oldest wood after flowering, to encourage an annual supply of new growth from the base; this will produce flowers in the following year. Do not cut out too much old wood.

Propagate by layering in spring, even though they may take 12 months to root.

Take care
Encourage young growths to develop from the base of the shrub. 134◗

Ruscus aculeatus
(Butcher's broom)

- **Tolerates dense shade**
- **Any type of soil**
- **Spring flowers; bright berries**

Besides 'Butcher's broom', *Ruscus aculeatus* is also known by at least eight other common names. It is called 'Butcher's broom' because it was used by butchers to wipe their blocks. This dwarf evergreen shrub, 45-90cm (18-36in) high, spreads freely by sucker growths springing from the base. The dark green, slightly glossy leaves of female plants have what are known as cladodes, ie the flower forms in the centre of the leaf, topped by a stiff spine at the apex. The dull-white flowers are produced in spring, and followed by sealing-wax-red berries provided male plants are available. The sexes are usually on separate plants, but there are some hermaphrodite forms.

There is probably no plant that does better when grown in dense shade. The only pruning needed is to cut out any dead or damaged shoots.

Propagate by division of the rootstock in spring.

Take care
Wear stout gloves when pruning.

Ruta graveolens 'Jackman's Blue'
(Rue)
- **Sunny position**
- **Any well-drained or lime-soil**
- **Summer flowering**

This evergreen shrub has been used both for cooking and for medicinal purposes, but today it makes a useful low-growing decorative shrub. The cultivar known as 'Jackman's Blue' has opalescent blue fern-like foliage, and dull yellow flowers are produced above the foliage during the summer. This shrub is grown more for its foliage than for its flowers; in fact, some growers remove the flower spikes as they appear. Bushes reach a height of 75cm-1m (30-39in) with a spread of 90cm-1.2m (3-4ft).

To keep bushes neat and tidy, prune them each spring by cutting back fairly severely to sound wood; at the same time remove the weaker growths.

Propagate by half-ripe cuttings in summer; insert in a cold frame.

Salix purpurea 'Pendula'
(Purple osier)
- **Full sun**
- **Any good garden soil, including lime and chalky soils**
- **Spring catkins**

This willow can be recommended for a small or medium-sized garden. Trained as a standard, it forms a wide spreading tree 2.5-3m (8-10ft) high; the pendulous branches have purple stems bearing a mass of tangled purple shoots and narrow leaves. Attractive slender catkins adorn the bare branches in early spring. Another willow of similar size is *Salix caprea* 'Pendula', the Kilmarnock willow. This female tree bears beautiful 'pussy' willow catkins in early spring, silky silver at first turning later to silvery green.

The only pruning needed for both of these weeping willows is to remove any shoots that arise on the stock that carries the grafted trees. Propagate by grafting onto stocks of *S. purpurea* and *S. caprea* respectively in spring.

Take care
Remove flower spikes if growing mainly for the colourful foliage. 135♦

Take care
Keep stocks clear of shoots.

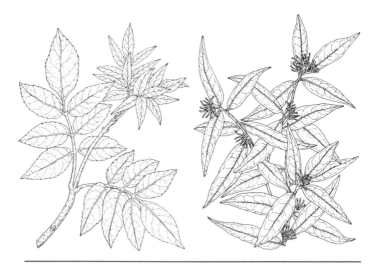

Sambucus nigra 'Aurea'

(Golden elder)
- **Full sun**
- **Any good garden soil**
- **Colourful foliage in summer**

Sambucus nigra 'Aurea' is a useful shrub that can light up a border. The foliage at first is greenish yellow, later changing to a golden-yellow which intensifies throughout the summer. It has large clusters of yellowish or dull white heavily fragrant flowers in summer followed by black berries, but it is the foliage for which it is grown. It usually reaches about 2m (6.5ft) high.

Even more striking is *S. racemosa* 'Plumosa Aurea', the golden cut-leaved elder. The species *S. racemosa* is the red-berried elder, but 'Plumosa Aurea' is grown for its deeply cut golden foliage. It has white flowers in spring, followed by red berries in autumn. This, too, will reach a height of 2m (6.5ft).

Both these elders can be pruned in spring, when they can be cut back to within a bud or two of the old wood. Propagate by taking hardwood cuttings in winter, inserted out of doors.

Take care
Remove any green shoots.

Sarcococca humilis

(Sweet box)
- **Tolerates heavy shade**
- **Any moist fertile soil**
- **Flowers in late winter or early spring**

This shrub is in no way related to the *Buxus* genus. It is a neat dwarf evergreen tufted shrub, densely branched and as a rule not more than 30-60cm (1-2ft) high. It has a suckering habit, not unlike butcher's broom, and is excellent for planting in groups as a ground cover plant. The narrow oval willow-like foliage is glossy green above but paler beneath; the leaves are 3-8cm (1.2-3.2in) long, and tapered at the apex. The axillary fragrant flowers are white with pink anthers, and are usually produced in spring, though at times they are to be found blooming in autumn or winter. The flowers are followed by blue-black berries.

No pruning is required, apart from the removal of old stems and any dead growth; do this after flowering has finished.

Propagate by division in spring or by hardwood cuttings in autumn inserted in an unheated frame.

Take care
Remove old and worn-out stems after flowering. 136◗

Senecio 'Sunshine'
- **Full sun**
- **Any soil**
- **Summer flowering**

This evergreen hardy flowering shrub is normally grown for its foliage rather than its flower. For many years it was known as *S. laxifolius* or *S. greyi*. It usually grows to 1-1.2m (3.3-4ft). It has leathery leaves up to 7cm (2.75in) long and 3cm (1.2in) wide; the young foliage has at first a cobweb-like grey covering above (later becoming smooth), with white felt beneath. In summer upright panicles of golden-yellow daisy-like flowers are produced.

This bushy shrub does well in coastal areas. If damaged by frost, bushes can be cut hard back in spring; carry out such pruning at least every four or five years. Heavy snow may weigh branches down; prune in spring to regain its normal shape.

Propagate by half-ripe cuttings in late summer or early autumn.

Take care
Keep these spreading bushes shapely by careful pruning. 136-7♦

Skimmia japonica
- **Sun or partial shade**
- **Fertile moist soil; not chalk soils**
- **Spring flowers; autumn and winter berries**

The hardy, evergreen shrub *Skimmia japonica* has several cultivars. Male and female flowers are on separate plants, and both sexes must be grown if berries are to be produced. *S.j.* 'Foremanii' is a female form and bears a profusion of bright scarlet berries. The yellowish green foliage has lance-like leaves 8cm (3.2in) long and 2cm (0.8in) wide and tapered at each end, with reddish stalks. This bushy spreading shrub does best in shade. It will reach 1-1.5m (3.3-5ft) tall and 1.5m (5ft) or more wide.

'Rubella' is a compact male clone with deep green foliage. It bears large conical flowerheads in spring and the panicles of ruby-red buds with their dark flower stalks are especially beautiful in winter. It reaches 1-1.2m (3.3-4ft) tall and equally wide. Propagate by seed sown in late winter, by half-ripe cuttings in summer, or by hardwood cuttings in autumn or early winter.

Take care
Plant both sexes for berries. 136♦

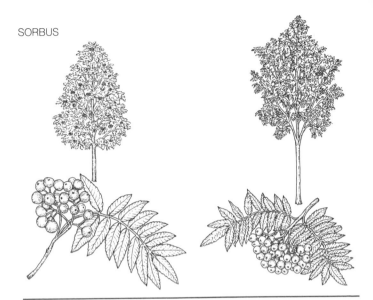

Sorbus commixta

- **Open sunny position**
- **Any well-drained fertile soil**
- **Spring flowers; autumn foliage and fruit**

This is the ideal tree where space is limited because of its ascending branches. At first it has a columnar habit but when fully mature it may spread a little. It can reach a height of 6-7.6m (20-25ft). The leaves are up to 25cm (10in) long, composed of six to eight pairs of leaflets. The young foliage is at first copper-coloured, later ageing to lustrous dark to medium green above, paler beneath. In winter it has long pointed buds of reddish brown, which may be sticky. The white flowers in spring are followed in autumn by large erect bunches of sealing-wax-red globular fruits or berries. In autumn the foliage is first deepish purple, changing to rich scarlet.

No pruning is required, provided the tree has been properly trained in early life. Avoid planting it in a thin soil over chalk.

Propagate by budding in summer, or by grafting in early spring.

Take care
Prepare the ground well before planting, and stake securely.

Sorbus 'Joseph Rock'

- **Open sunny position**
- **Any well-drained fertile soil**
- **Flowers in late spring or early summer; autumn foliage and fruits**

This small erect deciduous tree is a mountain ash of uncertain origin. It makes a superb addition to a small or medium-sized garden. In good soil it may reach 7.6m (25ft) high in 15 years, with a spread of 3m (10ft). The white flowers have creamy stamens and pink anthers. In autumn these give way to clusters of up to 50 fruits, at first greenish white before becoming creamy yellow to amber yellow, plus attractive autumn foliage in shades of purple, burnt orange, crimson and scarlet. The berries on the shaded side remain white, and hang on well into the winter; they do not seem to be attractive to birds.

No pruning is required, if the tree has been properly trained. Avoid thin soils over chalk, or trees will dry quickly at the roots in hot weather.

Propagate by budding in summer, or by grafting in early spring.

Take care
Prepare the ground well before planting, and stake securely.

Spartium junceum
(Spanish broom)
- **Full sun**
- **Any well-drained soil**
- **Flowers in summer and early autumn**

This erect hardy deciduous shrub has dark green rush-like stems and grows up to 3m (10ft) tall and 2.5m (8ft) wide. It is covered in large bright golden-yellow pea-shaped honey-scented flowers from early summer to early autumn. They are produced in terminal racemes, about 30cm (12in) long, on the current season's growth. The small leaves are inconspicuous. Grow Spanish broom beside a dark purple buddleia, also fragrant, for an unforgettable spectacle.

This is a useful shrub for growing in coastal areas, and does well on light chalky soils. It is easily raised from seed, but it dislikes root disturbance, so always use young pot-grown seedlings. Young plants need to be lightly pruned during the summer. Each year in late winter shorten young shoots on bushes that have flowered, to half or one-third of their length.

Propagate by seed sown in pots under glass in late winter.

Take care
Put out young plants.

Spiraea
Spring flowering
- **Sunny position**
- **Any good garden soil**
- **Spring flowering**

When dealing with spiraeas the problem is which to include; the four described here are hardy deciduous shrubs that flower in the spring. All are easily grown in any good garden soil, including chalk or lime soils.

The spring-flowering *S. × arguta* is a graceful branching shrub about 1.5-2m (5-6.5ft) high, with slender twiggy growth, and dainty pure white flowers produced in clusters on arching sprays of bloom. *S. media* is an erect shrub up to 1.2-2m (4-6.5ft) tall that bears long-stalked racemes of white flowers. *S. prunifolia* is the same height as *S. media*; the double white flowers in rosette-like clusters are borne along arching stems. Lastly, the pale green *S. thunbergii* has pure white flowers produced on wiry leafless stems in clusters of two to five; the shrub is about 90cm-1.5m (3-5ft) tall.

Once flowering has finished, remove old flowering shoots and shorten any long shoots. Propagate by half-ripe cuttings in summer.

Take care
Keep bushes shapely. 138♦

Spiraea
Summer flowering
- **Sunny position**
- **Any good garden soil**
- **Summer flowering**

The summer-flowering spiraeas are also hardy deciduous shrubs and easily grown. *S. × bumalda* 'Anthony Waterer' is 1.2-1.5m (4-5ft) high; above the dark green toothed leaves are flat branching clusters of carmine flowers 8cm (3.2in) wide, borne on the current season's growth from summer to autumn. In spring the cultivar 'Gold Flame' has unfolding leaves of rich bronze-red, later a light russet-orange, and crimson flowers in late summer. *S. nipponica* 'Snowmound' has small clusters of white flowers with green centres, each cluster borne at the end of a leafy twig on the previous year's growth; this shrub will reach a height of 1.2-1.5m (4-5ft). *S. × vanhouttei* is a 2m (6.5ft) vigorous shrub that is covered with umbels of pure white flowerheads in early summer.

Prune all these spiraeas fairly hard each year in late winter, reducing the previous year's growth to several eyes of the old wood. Propagate by half-ripe cuttings in summer.

Take care
Keep bushes within bounds.

Stachyurus praecox
- **Sun or semi-shade**
- **An acid humus fertile soil**
- **Late winter flowering**

A hardy deciduous flowering shrub that brightens gardens in late winter, when flowers – especially in the shrub border – are most welcome. The flowers are formed in autumn and open in late winter or very early spring. The oval lance-shaped leaves are 8-15cm (3.2-6in) long, lightly toothed at the margin and roughly half as wide. The stiff drooping racemes, 5-8cm (2-3.2in) long, are composed of from 12 to 20 cup-shaped greenish-yellow flowers, borne on the reddish-brown naked branchlets.

As frost can damage the flowers, choose a sheltered spot, in well-drained soil with plenty of humus. A sunny or semi-shaded position is best for this shrub. No regular pruning is needed.

Propagate, by layering or by half-ripe cuttings, in summer.

Take care
Give this species a sheltered position.

Staphylea colchica

(Bladder-nut)

- **Sun or semi-shade**
- **Any good fertile moist soil, including chalk or lime**
- **Flowers in spring**

This erect hardy deciduous shrub, 2-3m (6.5-10ft) tall, has bladder-like seed capsules, hence its common name Bladder-nut. The three- or five-leaflet foliage is darkish green above and lighter green beneath, and the margins have fine teeth. Each leaflet is approximately 6.5-8cm (2.5-3.2in) long. In spring the young shoots and lateral twigs have erect panicles of creamy white flowers among the leafy stems. Each cluster is up to 13cm (5in) long and wide. The flowers are followed later by two-or three-celled inflated capsules. If bushes become overgrown they can be cut back down to ground level during the winter, but the removal of an odd branch is best done immediately after flowering; usually no regular pruning is needed.

Propagate by seeds sown in late winter, or by half-ripe cuttings or layering during the summer.

Take care
Choose a moist, sunny or semi-shaded spot.

Stranvaesia davidiana

- **Full sun or partial shade**
- **Any good fertile soil**
- **Spring flowers, also foliage and berries**

An erect evergreen hardy shrub or small tree with glossy dark green leaves, 6.5-9cm (2.5-3.5in) long and 2.5cm (1in) wide. The leaves are often lightly tinted red in spring and crimson in autumn. It bears white flowers in spring, followed by clusters of scarlet hawthorn-like berries in autumn and winter. The attractive berries often remain on this evergreen for more than a year; for some reason birds do not appear to be attracted by them. Well established specimens will reach a height of 3.6-4.5m (12-15ft), and as much in width.

This shrub appears to flourish as well in a semi-shaded position as it does in full sun. It does well in most soils, but dislikes a dry situation and resents too chalky a soil. The only pruning needed is to thin crowded branches and shorten extra long shoots.

Propagate by seed, or by layering or half-ripe cuttings in autumn.

Take care
Allow this shrub plenty of space. 139♦

Styrax japonica

(Snowbell tree)
- **Sun or semi-shade**
- **Moist fertile lime-free soil**
- **Early summer flowering**

This handsome deciduous shrub or small tree, seldom taller than 5.5m (18ft), has oval leaves of a dark glossy green, and creamy white fuchsia-like flowers borne on short lateral shoots. As the flowers hang down, it is advisable to grow this species as a standard, so that one can look up at the pendent bell-like flowers. Shade it from early morning sun, as the young shoots and flower buds can be injured by frost.

This species needs moist loamy soil to which leaf-mould or moistened peat has been added. It is quite hardy except in frost-prone gardens. No regular pruning is necessary; and although an occasional thinning of overcrowded growth may be given, the natural beauty will be lost if it is pruned heavily.

Propagate by seeds sown out of doors as soon as ripe, by half-ripe cuttings in summer, or by layering in autumn.

Take care
Trees need a simple leader. 140-1▸

Syringa vulgaris

(Lilac)
- **Full sun**
- **Good fertile soil, including chalk soils**
- **Late spring to early summer flowering**

These hardy deciduous shrubs and small trees are renowned for their flowers and fragrance. Single varieties include 'Souvenir de Louis Spaeth', a deep wine red, flowering in mid-season; 'Maud Notcutt', with large pure white flowers, which last well when cut; 'Vestale', white, with light-green foliage; and 'Congo', lilac-red, free-flowering, and compact. Double varieties include 'Katherine Havemeyer', deep purple, large and strongly scented; 'Michael Buchner', lilac, with a lovely scent; 'Madame Lemoine', heavy white panicles; and 'Charles Joly', dark purplish red, with dark foliage.

Lilacs thrive on well-drained loamy soil or chalk; they dislike acid soils. Bushes can be as high as 5.5m (18ft). Plant them 3-4.5m (10-15ft) apart. Remove old flower trusses as soon as they are over, to prevent seed forming. No regular pruning is needed.

Propagate by layering in spring.

Take care
Remove suckers from grafted plants.

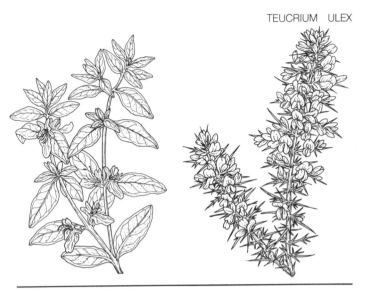

Teucrium fruticans

(Shrubby germander)
- **Full sun**
- **Light well-drained soil**
- **Flowers throughout summer**

This evergreen shrub is hardy in the open in mild localities, but in less favoured places it needs a sunny wall for protection. The white-covered square stems have small opposite oval leaves up to 4cm (1.6in) long, greyish green above and white-felted beneath, with a mint-like fragrance. Its lavender-blue flowers are produced in racemes 8-10cm (3.2-4in) long throughout the summer and into the autumn.

It produces the finest foliage when cut hard back in late winter or early spring; after such a slaughter very few flowers are produced, though there are plenty the following year. Bushes reach a height of 1.2m (4ft), and up to 2.1m (7ft) wide. The only pruning needed normally is to remove any surplus growth, or wood killed by frost in winter.

Propagate by half-ripe cuttings taken during the summer.

Take care
Protect plants if necessary.

Ulex europaeus

(Gorse)
- **Full sun**
- **Ordinary, poor dry or limy soil**
- **Flowers in spring**

The spine-tipped shoots and dark green foliage of this shrub are almost evergreen. Although gorse is at its best in spring, the golden-yellow fragrant flowers can be seen on bushes almost throughout the year. The cultivar 'Plenus' the double-flowered gorse, is slower growing than the common gorse, and more compact.

This hardy shrub grows happily in the bleakest of localities, and makes an excellent windbreak. Bushes can be badly frosted, but if they are cut back in spring, they will soon regenerate. Common gorse can grow up to 1.5m (5ft) tall; double gorse will reach a height of only 1.2m (4ft). As this genus transplants badly, it is best to put out pot-grown plants.

Propagate the common gorse by seed sown out of doors in spring. The double cultivar does not produce seed; cuttings must be taken from the current year's growth during the summer months.

Take care
Keep bushes under control 141◆

Viburnum × bodnantense

- Sunny position
- Any good fertile soil
- Flowers in autumn and winter

This vigorous deciduous flowering shrub is a hybrid between *V. farreri (V. fragrans)* and *V. grandiflorum*. It appears to sulk for a few years at first, but once established there is no holding it. The frost-resistant hybrid named 'Dawn' has buds that are at first rose-red, and then open into clusters of sweetly fragrant rose-tinted white flowers on the naked branches, followed by deep green foliage with red stalks. The height of this hybrid is around 2.5-3m (8-10ft), sometimes more.

When pruning is needed, remove complete old or weak branches at ground level; this will encourage new growth from the base.

Propagate by layering; rooted branches often layer naturally, otherwise layers can be put down during early summer.

Take care
Give this viburnum ample space to spread itself. 140-1♦

Viburnum plicatum 'Mariesii'

- Prefers partial shade
- Any moist fertile soil
- Flowers in late spring and early summer

This deciduous horizontal-branched flowering shrub seems happier with some shade, rather than in full sun. The oval pointed leaves are toothed except at the base, 5-10cm (2-4in) long, up to 6.5 (2.5in) wide, dull dark green above, pale greyish beneath, and slightly downy. Bushes can be 1.5-3m (5-10ft) high, and wider, so this shrub must be given room to spread. The large inflorescences have ray flowers about 4.5cm (1.8in) wide with the pinhead fertile flowers in the centre, held on stalks about 6.5cm (2.5in) long. The foliage in autumn turns to dull crimson or purplish red.

No regular pruning is needed. Propagate by summer layering, or by half-ripe cuttings of the current year's growth taken in summer.

Take care
Allow this lovely shrub plenty of room to stretch itself. 142♦

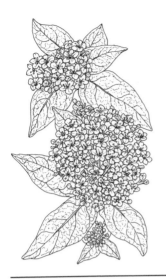

Viburnum tinus

(Laurustinus)
- **Full sun or partial shade**
- **Any good garden soil, including chalk**
- **Winter and spring flowers**

An evergreen flowering shrub that makes a dense rounded bush. The opposite leaves, dark glossy green above and paler beneath, are borne on red stalks; the main shoots are red above, green beneath and warted. At the ends of the leafy shoots are terminal flower clusters 5-10cm (2-4in) across. The greeny buds are tinged with mauvy pink before opening white in winter and spring, followed by deep blue fruits that become black. Bushes will reach a height of 2-3.6m (6.5-12ft). The cultivar 'Eve Price' is of more compact habit, with smaller leaves.

Laurustinus does well on chalk or non-chalk soils and is excellent in coastal areas. Prune bushes that have grown out of hand or are frost damaged by cutting them hard back to the oldest wood near ground level in late spring.

Propagate by seed sown in late winter, or by half-ripe heel cuttings taken in early to late summer.

Take care
Allow to grow naturally. 143♦

Weigela hybrids

- **Full sun**
- **Rich fertile soil, including chalk**
- **Summer flowering**

These are trouble-free deciduous flowering shrubs of which there are a number of attractive hybrids. The flowers are similar to those of honeysuckle except that all are scentless. Hybrids that are usually available include: 'Abel Carriere', a deep rosy carmine with a yellow throat, and a strong grower that can be 2m by 2m (6.5ft by 6.5ft); 'Bristol Ruby', a bright ruby red with almost black buds, fairly upright in habit, 2m by 1.5m (6.5ft by 5ft); 'Candida', pure white with bright green foliage, 2m by 2m (6.5ft by 6.5ft) or even wider; and 'Newport Red', bright red.

They are all easily grown, provided they have rich soil with ample moisture at their roots. Prune regularly as soon as they have finished flowering, and then remove old flowering side branches. Overgrown bushes can be cut hard back in spring.

Propagate by hardwood cuttings in autumn, inserted out of doors.

Take care
Prune annually after flowering. 144♦

Yucca flaccida 'Ivory'

- Full sun
- Any soil, especially sandy loam
- Summer flowering

Zenobia pulverulenta

- Sun or partial shade
- Cool lime-free moist loamy or peaty soil
- Early summer flowering

This low-growing evergreen hardy flowering shrub with its architectural foliage helps to create a subtropical atmosphere in the garden. The bluish green leaves are 3-4.5cm (1.2-1.8in) wide. The long spikes of creamy white bells are poised horizontally – unlike most yuccas, whose flowers hang down. The bells are borne at right angles on 1.2m (4ft) long stems, and they have well-formed pointed petals. This is an ideal plant for the gardener who has limited space.

No pruning is necessary. Propagate by division. Alternatively, the tops can be induced to root by trimming off half the leaves and inserting the stems in earthenware pots filled with a sandy compost; place them in a greenhouse.

This ericaceous deciduous or semi-evergreen shrub is entirely on its own, as *Z. pulverulenta* is the only species in the genus *Zenobia*. It will grow to a height of 1.2-2m (4-6.5ft). The alternate oval-shaped leaves, tapering at the base and rounded at the apex, are a bluish green, sometimes tinged with rosy pink. The pure white bell-like pendent flowers are produced in early summer.

The only pruning needed is to cut off the spent blossoms as soon as they have faded. Occasionally poor or weak plants should have the old wood cut back to encourage new growth. Apply a mulch of moistened peat or leaf-mould. Propagate by half-ripe cuttings placed in gentle heat in summer, or by layering in autumn.

Take care
Give correct soil conditions, and do not let plants become dry at the roots in very hot dry summers.

Take care
Yuccas need a sunny aspect.

Index of Common Names

Potentilla 'Elizabeth'

Credits

Line artwork
The drawings in this book have been prepared by Maureen Holt
© Salamander Books Ltd.

Photographs
The majority of the photographs in this book have been taken by Eric Crichton. © Salamander Books Ltd.

Copyright in the following photographs belong to the suppliers:

Eric Crichton: 12(B), 13, 16(T), 34(T), 35(T), 36, 38(B), 38-9(B), 43, 45, 47, 68(B), 70(B), 71(B), 72(T), 73(T), 75(B), 76(B), 77(B), 78(B), 78-9, 80(B), 103(B), 105(B), 106(B), 111(T), 129, 133(T), 135, 136(B), 136-7, 139, 140-1(T), 141, 144.
Michael Warren: 6, 44, 130, 131.

Editorial assistance
Copy-editing and proof-reading:
Maureen Cartwright